# This Book's Not Perfect

# Not Perfect

## But Neither Are We

## Robin Lambert

Gesund Publishing

314 Dawn Avenue

Woodstock, Virginia 22664

ISBN 978-0-9986415-1-5

https://www.facebook.com/gesundpublishing/

Visit the author's website at https://EarthToRobin.com

First Edition

This is a work of creative nonfiction. While all the stories in this book are 99.9% almost true… in a way, some names and identifying details have been changed to protect the privacy of the people involved.

*Dedicated to my Mom and Dad*

# Preface

This book is a personal memoir depicting various events experienced during my lifetime. It does not include the 'meaning of life' or attempt to answer all the questions that we ask ourselves during life-changing moments. It is not meant to be a self-help book, but it did begin as a help to myself. There are various topics recalled, in the stories that are told, which are of great significance to me. The Importance of Family. The Beauty of Giving. Coping with Death. Being Human. Everything told through dozens of memories from my 50-plus years here on Earth.

But I don't believe that the words will come across as sad or sappy. Many readers "really enjoy" my stories, so apparently, the occasional bad language or risqué situation is taken for what they are, an everyday part of life. Not a cheap selling point.

I was going to include the chapter "Why I Write", but that's not important. Plus, that chapter could have been wrapped up in sixteen words. Man's Best Friend dies. Man inadvertently tries to die. Man gets better by writing silly stories.

Hopefully, what you'll get from this book, is the enjoyment that comes from reading, a laugh or three after relating to a tale, an occasional warm and fuzzy feeling, and a strong urge to be nice to others.

# Table of Contents

# Chapter One - Childhood

## *Catherine*

Have you ever had one of those days when everything seems to go wrong? The world's just out to get you. No matter how hard you try to go up, life always seems to drag you back down?

For two months-short of a decade, I worked at a conference and retreat center for the Episcopal Diocese of Virginia, tucked away in the hills of The Shenandoah Valley. I began work there on a very part-time basis, working around my attempts at a career as a solo fishing guide. Food service and fishing, that's a pretty good gig. But then two days in the kitchen turned into six and time with a fly rod in my hand became scarce. I woke up one day and found myself hiring, training and scheduling an entire kitchen staff. Developing new recipes, planning menus and ordering food for up to 6000 meals a week. If you're going to do something, do it right. Whether it was playing a game, building a business, or simply screwing up, I've always seemed to succeed.

Every year at the retreat, there is a special weekend gathering known as "Family Camp". A special time of the year which is host to hordes of families... grandparents, moms, dads, and kids...for a week chock-full of special programs, fresh air, and of course, great food.

Over the course of several years, I had gotten to know a young woman named Catherine. She was probably thirteen or fourteen at this point. I don't remember the reason, but she is forever confined to a wheelchair. Her Mom carts her into the dining hall every day, always after most of the guests have left, perhaps to escape the crowds and stares, probably just for the ease of maneuvering around the empty chairs. Catherine reclines sprawled out in her wheelchair. Her hands and feet are stretched outwards, with a slight, painful-looking twist. Sort of like an extreme arthritis patient, but her taunt limbs are probably the result of her tendons having gone haywire. Catherine looks at you out of the corner of her eyes. Initially it seems that she doesn't trust you, but that's just the way she looks at things. She wears a bib at mealtime, her

Mom spoon feeds her cut up bits of meats and coarser foods, she paws the mashed potatoes and veggies, successfully getting them in the general area of her mouth.

Some people speak and make no sense what so ever. Catherine doesn't speak at all. But she makes a lot of sense with different gestures of her tiny, constricted body. If her Mom serves her up a spoonful of something that she doesn't like, the arms start a flailing, rejected morsels are drooled out and she angrily backhands them to the floor. To express her excitement as I neared her table, her permanently extended body would start flopping in her chair, her skinny legs kicked out of control, and she'd extend her right arm towards me, the palm of her frail hand always facing down. Not because she was trying to be elegant, but because that's how you reach out to hold another's hand when your own arm doesn't rotate. So, I'd hold hands with Catherine, her hands still slimy with mashed potatoes and pureed carrots. And selfishly, deep down inside, I'd think to myself that I must be the nicest person ever to have walked on the face of this Earth, after being so attentive to this young woman. On the last weekend that I saw Catherine, she held out her hand, always shaking like an old woman, and we shared another handshake. That shaky hand guided mine towards her face and she kissed the back of my hand. When you're humbled down to this level, it becomes hard to see over the tray attached to her wheelchair.

So, when my damn shoulder hurts or I missed watching the big ballgame on TV last night for some stupid reason, I try to remember the lessons that Catherine has taught me.

Often it seems that the people that we look down upon and question why, are in fact the ones that we should look up to for simple, honest answers.

## *Andrew*

The Christmas Season isn't the best time of year for many a sad soul. While seemingly everyone delights at the commercial symbols of Christmas, others feel an opposite emotion.

I never spoke with my son outside of the confines of his Mother's womb. Perhaps the lack of a voice to remember relieves me of one less thing on which to grieve. I'm lucky, I suppose. The less, the better.

His Mother was as wacky as I am when it comes to lucky numbers and other superstitions. In choosing the child's name, a formula of specific letters and an exact total number of letters (which even I never understood) was used by her/we to derive at the boy's name. His first name would be Andrew.

I'm probably putting too much value into this whole "Divine Power or Coincidence" struggle of thoughts that I feel from time to time. I sometimes wonder if I'm just going crazy and there's a big "Conspiracy of Silence" amongst everyone else to shield me from realizing my own insanity.

After spending the first eighteen years of life going to church every Sunday, I deviated way-off course, and went on a big spree of Sin for thirty-years. After my near-death experience of last year, it's not like I saw a glaring light from above and suddenly decided to run for Pope of Virginia, but I can't help but take notice of seemingly inexplicable events from both the past and the present. Yes, most things happen for a reason, but simply applying logical reasoning doesn't help explain certain things to me.

Last month, my sister asked if I'd like to join her in a long overdue Encore Performance by joining our church's choir during a traditional Christmas program. The two of us in that Church again, after so many years, should've been cause for an early snow storm. Or locusts. Or lightning. But it seemed like the right thing to do. My Mom would be elated, an early

Christmas present for her. And more powerful was my Aunt's presence in this year's program. Currently battling cancer, she continued a string of appearances that began forty-years ago.

I hadn't sung in public (invited) since I was a Senior in High School. I secretly had moments when a case-of-the nerves would develop, so I began a mental list of calming thoughts. The sheet music was distributed during the first week of practice. On the cover of one sheet that I was given, a song which was my Mother's favorite, was written in pencil the name Howard. In 1976, I had stood in the choir next to my Uncle Howard. This old sheet music had once been his own copy.

My Aunt was an obvious go-to when seeking a calming influence to fight any nerves. At various times during the weeks of practice sessions, I'd have the unsettling thought of *"Can I even do this?"*. A little glance over my left shoulder and two rows up, and I could see my Aunt. And those questions were answered.

Four days before the final dress rehearsal, I had a few extra nerves placed on my shoulders, just in case I had calmed the others. The choir would enter the darkened sanctuary through a side door. Myself and a member of the Junior

Choir, would lead all the choir members into the church and assist the women up the steps of the performance platform.

The afternoon of the final rehearsal was the first time that I would meet the members of the Junior Choir. The rehearsal was open to the public and a small group of spectators had gathered throughout the pews. As we lined-up in the hallway before the big entrance, I thought of how nervous these children in the choir must be. As I first met the young man who would enter the church with me, I made a point of politely introducing myself, perhaps it might calm any nerves that he might have.

*"Hello, my name is Robin"* bending down as I extended my hand for a man-to-man handshake.

He took my hand, then looked up from behind long brown bangs, with big brown eyes and politely said...

*"Hello, my name is Andrew"*

My heart said *"Of course it is"*, but my mouth could not speak.

From where I stood, the weekend went perfectly. That young man may never understand the good deed he did that day, but I will never forget.

## *The Gift*

Merriam-Webster Dictionary defines 'gift' as

1)        a notable capacity, talent, or endowment

2)        something voluntarily transferred by one person to another without compensation

3)        the act, right, or power of giving

During the span of my life, I have given many gifts and I have received many gifts. And quite honestly, very few of those gifts that I gave or the gifts that I received were all that memorable. Maybe the memories of gifts last for a few years, or maybe for a few months, or maybe just a few weeks. A very few gifts are etched into my mind forever.

Years ago, I gave a young woman my last five dollars. Not from the savings account that I didn't have at the time. Not on a rubber check. It was the wrinkled five-dollar-bill that was in my left front pocket. She was in an abusive relationship. Her lesser half beat on her, checked in on her regularly at her work and controlled all the family's money. He lived comfortably on their two paychecks. She worried, on that significant day, that she might not have enough gasoline to get her son to daycare and her to work. So, I gave her my five-dollar bill. She said *"You're the nicest person that I know"*. And she didn't even realize that the five dollars was my life savings up until that point.

Why in the hell would I do something like that? Back in those days, I could've bought a pack of smokes and a six-pack of beer with my five dollars. Throughout my lifetime, I've led a self-centered existence. But there were occasional bright moments of hope, where it was all about someone else and not just about myself. When you think of Christmas now a days, you think of gift giving. The Scrooge in me sees the typical family sitting around in a big circle, each member throwing a twenty-dollar bill into the middle, everyone reaching in for a twenty, and then thanking another family member for the nice 'twenty' that they had just received. Wow, that certainly was cynical. But again, why in the hell would I give away my last five dollars?

When my sisters and I were kids, Christmas was a big deal. Our family wasn't living in anybody's lap of luxury. But our Mom and Dad went out of their way to provide us with everything that we needed. Sure, we ate our share of Brussels sprouts, navy beans, and scrapple, each served with ketchup, the condiment of the decade. But we ate well, we lived in a nice home and we were very fortunate. And it took me many years to realize the other thing that we children were…which was grateful. At Christmas time, our family, like so many other families, had a routine for the season. A holiday routine that was our own tradition. Not TRADITION! like some Russian fiddler on a rooftop, but typical things like opening one gift on Christmas Eve, church on Christmas morning, and eating some German inspired strudel-thingy before opening the remaining gifts.

Early on one special Christmas morning, we had followed tradition to a tee, leaving a trail of giggles and wrapping paper in the living room. The three of us had taken in quite a haul of gifts that morning, much more than we deserved. It seemed that the madness was over for yet another year. Then the announcement was made that there was one more gift to open and we were directed towards the closed doors of the formal dining room (which we rarely used). And behind those doors was a memory waiting to be etched into my memory forever. Brand new bikes for my sisters and myself. Our parents had rubbed a couple of coins together and gave us something special. Not just special like a new bike on Christmas morning kind of special, but a gift that we could use throughout our lives.

*"You're the nicest person that I know"*. Well, I may not have been the best of student, but I had great teachers.

## *Boys will be Boys*

I grew up with a healthy dose of Mad Magazine for reading material, having skimmed right over "Run Spot Run" and landing plumb in the middle of "Spy vs. Spy". My Mom has always said that I "walk to the beat of a different drummer", a comforting, perhaps complimentary phrase that might explain my history of actions that "consciously adopt a different approach or attitude from most people". And I blame some of those tendencies squarely on the cartoon shoulders of Alfred E. Neuman, the boy without a care in the world.

When I was eleven years old, I joined a local radical Eco terrorist group. Fifty years ago, my parents built the very first house in an area of our town that is now cluttered with street after street of single family homes. The neighborhood of my youth wasn't actually a neighborhood at all in the beginning, but one lone house surrounded by fields full of bugs, two ponds full of frogs and new home construction sites full of little wires with caps attached that blasting crews had left behind. The first pond on the street was drained and gone before anyone had even noticed, bulldozed into a flat front lawn for the Patterson's new home. But months later, when the town's maintenance department started to drain the second pond, a string of tin cans began to chatter. Our tight knit group of well-intended militants sprang into action. During the daytime hours of 9 to 5, the town's workers devised a drainage system, a series of PVC pipes, which ran from the pond sanctuary to the newly laid sewer system. After dinner, the counter-attack began. Rambo hadn't been born yet, so in lieu of face paint, bandannas, and Bowie knives, we headed out into the darkness clad in Wrangler jeans, flannel shirts, and a shroud of determination. During the day, the pond slowly lost water, the banks began to grow. At night, eleven-year-old commandos clogged the pipes to stop the flow of life-giving water. Day after day, the battle ensued until our pond was no more. The Man had won, despite our acts of valor. Not to be a conspiracy theorist, but I still think that there was dirty (muddy) money being passed between the building contractor and the town council when it came time to 'purchase' that new home's building permit. Ergo, the etymology of the term 'Hush' money; as we crawled along the pond's muddy bank and someone broke the silence by cracking a fallen tree branch; everyone else would loudly whisper *"Hush!"*

Because that's what boys do.

Among the wooded area that now lines an Interstate highway, there lies a series of cave openings, hidden by a web of vines and brush. We'd try to gain entrance into the underworld by tearing away at the thick vegetation, but only exposed holes the size of our heads and never made it underground. Those blasting caps would have probably come in handy, but we weren't that smart.

With our pond's water now flowing through the pipes of the town sewer, the neighborhood's growing number of kids quickly learned how to put the town's water supply to different sources of entertainment. In the summer, we sprayed gallons of water onto the backyard of my house, the soil already soggy from a cracked septic tank. Nothing spells fun like tackle football in a pool of teeming bacteria. The mother of my buddy from across the street was my math teacher at school. The morning after one of our football games, she began math class by threatening me in front of our entire class. "If my son EVER comes home looking like that again, you're doing our laundry!" I was never very good at math. I don't think that I got an "A" that year.

One winter, while home from school because of snow, we were enjoying the parent-less afternoon with hours of snow sledding. We used the Plum family's garden hose to

13

spray down the blacktopped road on which we lived. The ice that formed created a wicked fast luge surface, doubling our normal speed, but was frowned upon for some reason by our parents as they slid home from work.

Because that's what boys do.

Evel Knievel was a hero to many a young boy during my childhood. At my friend, Mitch's house, over on Susan Avenue, a poster of Evel graced his bedroom wall. I can still see the red, white, and blue caped daredevil popping a wheelie on his stunt motorcycle, a man's man, and a misguided source of inspiration. The sight of your idol, on a two-wheeled gasoline-powered machine, flying across a row of buses, was enough to cause a young boy to do some really crazy things. With a couple of cinder blocks and a few 2"X 6" boards, you could create your own ramp and jettison your spider bike across the Caesar's Palace fountain in your backyard. Despite the complete lack of helmets and knee-pads, the worst injuries came from the crushing of little family jewels against the bike's banana seat during the impact of landing.

On a side note: If you're an eleven-year-old boy, DO NOT use the bag of lime from the family's shed to line your wiffle ball field in the back yard. Your Dad won't appreciate it.

For decades, MAD was the most successful magazine to publish free of advertising. Their satirical advertisements would one day become classics, but they may have been a little bit too 'deep' for an eleven-year-old to appreciate. But in the back pages of The Hulk or The Silver Surfer comic books, you'd find things that us boys could have only dreamed of owning. A pair of X-Ray glasses came with the chance to see the bones of your own hand. But what we really wanted to know was if it would work on a classmate's dress, while she crunched and squealed as she tried to cover her privates. The Charles Atlas Training Program could eliminate bullies from our lives. Learn to throw your voice and drive your teacher crazy. Become a famous artist by submitting your sketch of a cute, baby deer. Thrill in lighting a couple of Magic Black Snakes to watch 'em smoke and grow. With an envelope, an 8-cent stamp, and 2 one dollar bills, you could become the proud owner of a family of sea monkeys or the commander of 100 plastic Army soldiers.

My buddy up the street bought himself a super-duper, Space-age magnifying glass. Not the type that Grandpa would use to read the newspaper. It was a 10"X10" sheet of hard Plexiglas, with ominous circles of etchings that decreased in size to a pin-point in the middle. If you held that sucker up with two hands to the sun at the correct angle, the concentrated light beam contained enough localized energy that it would burn stuff. A lot of different stuff. We didn't invent the pastime, but you could really wreak havoc on a hill of ants. And other bugs. And leaves. And anything else that you could think of.

So, we're out in the field behind our houses, enjoying the bright, sunny, dry summer day. Today's operation was focused on the Ninja-like assault of pesky grasshoppers. With high levels of silence and stealth, you could get within a foot of an enemy grasshopper. Even if the subject sensed you and scurried to the backside of a blade of grass, he was no match for The Glass. Later, during the onslaught, my buddy accidentally set smolder to a small batch of dried grass. Harmless to begin with, a fire began to grow as he tried to tamp it out with his tennis shoes. *"Help me put it out!"* So, I joined in on the effort, as the ring of smoke and flicker of flames grew to eight or ten feet wide. Our frantic yelling and the increasing smoke caught the attention of my friend's father, Pastor of the local Lutheran Church. He came to our rescue armed with a shovel and we continued the fight. As the diameter of burning brush reached twenty feet, the faint sound of emergency sirens could be heard over the crackling of flames. Our volunteer fire department soon took over and quickly put an end to the disaster. I began the long walk of shame to my house. Like many of the other neighbors, my parents were at the edge of their lawn, trying to figure out what all the commotion was about. As I walked by, chin down, they asked *"What's goin' on up there?"* I kept walking. Directly to my bedroom cell where I knew that I'd be incarcerated.

### Bikes Hikes

Back when I was ten, eleven, maybe twelve years old, me and my best friend would plan bike hikes, usually on a Saturday morning, to explore different local attractions. But not the ones that you'd find in a travel brochure. Back in a time when you might tell a parent that "I'm going over to Mitch's house" and then take off on your spider bike, no helmet, no knee pads, no money, no cell phone, and best of all, no worries. And the parent would reply *"uh... yeah... O.K... have fun!"* You needed no GPS because you already thought that you knew where you were going because you had planned it in math class on Wednesday.

We did this on a regular basis. Mitch was much more in tune with motorcycle gangs than I was at this time of our

Robin Lambert

lives. Depending upon how many friends had joined us for the day, our imitation of the Hell's Angels grew to an intimidating number of bikers, maybe six or seven, dependent upon who hadn't finished their chores that day. We'd cruise the streets of our hometown, ignoring any safe biking rules that were in place at the time. *"Get your spider bikes runnin' 'Head on down the highway!"* One magnificent day, only three bikers showed. Mitch, our friend John, and myself. Destination? The town dump. It was a magical, mystical wonderland. At least for a twelve-year-old boy. We had one very powerful slingshot, three bikes, no bottled water, and no snack foods. So, we only stayed seven hours. The dump was a dump. But it had highlights that you just didn't find in your own backyard. Number one was rats. Number two was big tubed televisions. Lastly, and most interesting at the time, syringes, and blood samples from the local hospital. Yep, they just dropped off the evil waste at the dump for a few twelve-year-olds with which to play. So, we spent the day blowing up T.V.'s with a slingshot (they used to explode), killing rats and perhaps injecting dead rats with Mrs. Smith's blood sample syringe. Yeah, yeah, we all became mass murderers.

The more consistent run of our biker group was a trip to the Woodstock observation tower. A quick five-mile ride out

18

of town, on your spider bike, with no helmet, no knee pads, no money, no cell phone, across Burnshire's Dam bridge, to the base of the mountain. Then up the winding mountain road, which took you to an elevation of 2000 feet. It tires me to think of it now but back then we'd basically push our bikes up the side of the mountain. It was steep, the road just winded back and forth, back and forth. And it was summer, dammit! As you neared the top, there was fresh spring water spewing out of a steel pipe, sticking out of the mountainside. Reaching this point was accomplishment number one. You knew that you were close. Next, a short hike by foot to the tower. I looked it up, the tower is 298 feet tall. I think that I was five feet tall. So up we went, three flights of stairs to the top platform. We didn't realize it then but this is where you come to see the famous Seven Bends of the Shenandoah River. But that's not why we came here on this treacherous journey. We were twelve-year-old boys. So, we pissed off the tower. We spit, repeatedly, off the tower. And like so many that came before us, with pocketknives, we etched our initials and other things into the wood of the tower. But that was the boring part of the day. Next, the descent.

The road was partially graveled, but mostly just dusty, especially in summer. Hootin' and hollerin' as we started down the mountain, you picked up speed really fast.

Fortysomething-year-old memories are sketchy at best, but I swear on my spider bike's seat that our friend Jay, on one particular day, came down that mountain with little or no brakes. Just Chuck Taylor tennis shoes, dragging his feet during the rough patches, going too fast through the rest.

I remember parts of the trip down the mountain as relaxing. One day, we had twenty something deer cut across the road in front of us. We sat still and watched them disappear into the silence of the woods. Then there were the terrifying parts. Like the straight stretch of road that we knew as the "rumble strips", limestone ridges exposed from soil erosion, where your knees had to act as shock absorbers while your butt still took a beating. And Jay was still dragging his feet.

When we got back to the bridge, there was nothing but giggling and laughing. We were stupid. We were twelve-year-old boys. As the gang got back to town, we had accomplished something that no one else had done that day. And we were better off for it. At the end of the day, we went our separate ways. *"Hi Mom… yeah, I was just out with the guys for a ride"*. If she only knew.

Lastly, the trip to the Little Wolf Hole. There are two Wolf Holes. One big, one little. They're local swimming holes outside of our town. The Big Wolf Hole is quite visible from a main road, people bring lawn chairs, etc. The Little Wolf Hole, well you gotta know where it is. You drive far out into the country and then you take a left. Into the woods. Back in the day, during the spring time, potentially scary people would just hang out, drink beer, smoke things and carry rocks back up from downstream after the spring thaw, damming the waters that formed the swimming hole.

So, Mitch, John and myself are probably twelve at the time. Skipping town for the day. Spider bikes, no helmets, no knee pads, no money, no cell phones. The road is a two-lane major backroads thoroughfare, connecting the smaller towns and communities. From town to the Little Wolf Hole is probably twelve miles. So, we're cruising along, our little knees pumping, minding ourselves, dodging occasional traffic. When out of the corner of our eyes did appear a large German Shepherd, sprinting in our direction, a continuous growl coming from behind a big set of large fangs. I wasn't paying attention that day in school, but apparently waking a large dog from a peaceful sleep gives him a really crappy attitude. See kids, back in our day, dogs weren't always restricted at home. As a matter of survival, the knee pumping hit hyper-speed. The dog was probably as big as any one of us. Just as death seemed a certainty, the Shepherd came to the end of his chain. A loud yelp, he flipped in the air, and we laughed. And we laughed and laughed, our knee pumping pace greatly reduced. We hung out at the Little Wolf Hole, jumped into the cool water, even road our bikes into the water.

The stream running into the Wolf Hole is a trout stream, so the water is very cool and refreshing. Eventually it was time to go, so off we went on our trek back to town. We're peddling along and again we come upon that same dumbass dog. Laughing we were until we realized that he was no longer chained. Knee pumping back up to hyper-speed. The Shepherd's nipping at John's ankles. We're going faster and faster. Then the Shepherd finally loses interest.

Moral of that story. You don't have to outrun the Shepherd. Just outrun your friends?

## Little League Baseball

Build it and they will come. The ball park of my youth was a block from my house, next to the town's public swimming pool and picnic shelters. A hand operated scoreboard, a grounds crew composed of volunteers, small wooden bleachers standing just off the first and third base lines. I was signed as a walk-on, straight out of the third grade, after honing my skills in the bush league of my backyard. Snagging self-propelled fly balls had finally paid off.

The park's only restrooms were 300 yards from the diamond. Behind the home plate area was a pebbled concrete water fountain, whose rusting faucet provided a refreshing drink of warm water throughout the summer season. I don't remember any concession stand food because that wasn't important. What was important was winning.

Other than the simple, concrete dugouts, the only building structure at our stadium was the wooden announcer's box, located directly behind of home plate. This building would in time become known as "Punky's Palace". Punky Reilly was and will always be the area's number one sports fan. He was a "special" man before there was a politically correct term for "special". Kids can be cruel and may have occasionally made fun of him, but usually they just flocked around him. A Piped Piper of sports fanatics, his glass was always full. *"That Luray team sure was sump'n the other night. Don't you worry, we'll get 'em next time".* The only reason that he'd miss a Central High School game, home or away, was if there were two different sports playing on the same night. During the fourth inning stretch of our Little League games, the kids would all run to the door of Punky's Palace, excitedly begging for the honor of collecting league donations from the evening's crowd. He was the only voice that I can remember ever announcing a little league ballgame and is forever honored on a plaque in the high school's wall of sports trophies.

There were six teams in the league that season of my rookie year. I played center field for the powerhouse Woodstock Lions. Our ball caps and stirrups were a fierce color of yellow and our cleats were dirty Chuck Taylors. As young 'men in the making', we learned about rules, structure, and how to succeed in life. All from a little leather-covered ball. No ribbons were awarded to anyone. When you lost a contest, you felt bad. The coaches taught you how to succeed the next time. Practice, hard work and using your noggin'. There were no team managers named 'Jim'. I was taught by MR. Danley and COACH Hoover. 'Yes, SIR' was the answer to a coach's instruction. The only doping allegations that season involved a package of Pop Rocks and a bottle of Coca-Cola.

If our pitching rotation was working to our advantage, our ace Greg would be on the mound against any of the stronger teams in our league. Greg had physically sprouted earlier than any other member of our team. He was heads above us in height and in God-given baseball talent. But he wasn't a chiseled Adonis, but more of a Babe Ruth figure, with boyish charm and chubby cheeks. The black hair emphasized the smile's white teeth, like film images of Ruth before a game. Relaxed, confident, always talking and cracking jokes as he tossed a ball around with a teammate. But as the contest began, the expressions changed to the teeth-grinding look of a restrained Rottweiler before an organized dog fight. Of his repertoire of pitches, he only used one. That was the fastball. And the deception of his fastball had nothing to do with its velocity, but the location of his pitches. Sure, the ball may have been screaming at 70 mph during the 46-foot reentry flight. But its final destination was the key to his success. Randomly, the ball might embed itself ten feet high into the steel, chain-linked fence or singe the earlobe of a batter, sending him slumping to the safety of the dirt. But more times than not, it popped into the brave, waiting mitt of our catcher. The infield chatter started..." *Hey batter, batter, batter...hey batter, batter"* As he began his windup, the crowd would collectively hold its breath. Then 0.407 seconds later, they would react with laughter, a shudder of fear, or more often than not, a round of applause.

In the position of right outfield, Charlie Brown had Lucy. Abbott & Costello had Nobody. Of course, we had a right fielder as well. I shall call him "Bill". Because his name was Bill. The position of right field on a Little League team was often stereotyped by different characteristics. First off, someone had to field the position, anyone. The least athletically gifted were usually elected by default. Most opposing batters were right handed and bat swinging mechanics sent most fly balls to left or center field. Manning the right field position appeased the parents and added a notch to your athletic resume. But right fielders were often Dreamers, not Followers. Before the crack of the bat, I would have compiled my list of cat-like reactions to the different scenarios that might unfold. If it was a short single over the shortstop's head, I'm firing the ball home to throw out the runner leaving third. A long fly-out ensures the runner from third will score, so I'm going to second and hold the tagging runner at first. The right fielder was wondering why potato butterflies have black spots on their white wings; why don't they shoo when you kick at them; why are they out here in right field anyways; don't see no potatoes around anywhere and no flowers either, except for those dandelions over there by that umpire man.

It was the bottom of the sixth, the final inning of a Little League game. Greg's standing tall on the mound, protecting our 2-1 lead. There were two outs, with enemy runners on first and third. Coming to bat is one of the weaker batters from the opposing team. Excited screams of encouragement came from the opposing grandstands. *"Just make contact, buddy! You're due...it's your time!"* *"Three more strikes Greg, three more strikes!"* Rockwell couldn't have painted a scene to match the excitement of just being there. Like Patton out maneuvering Rommel at the battle of El Guettar, Coach Hoover began repositioning his defensive troops, going in for the kill.

*"Jay, watch the bunt, watch the bunt!!!"* Coach hollered

*"OUTFIELD IN! OUTFIELD IN!"* as he frantically motioned arm signals.

A passing airplane had caught the attention of Bill.

*"BILL, COME IN! FURTHER! COME IN!"*
*"All right Greg, ONE MORE STRIKEOUT, BABY! ONE MORE! BRING THE HEAT!"*

After two slightly wild pitches, Greg settled down and delivered back to back fireballs of perfection. The parents were at a point where acting the fool was not a concern; just scream 'til your lungs hurt. The electricity in the air was so dense, that lightning bolts cracked in the mountains on an otherwise clear day. Greg became a living monument on the mound; a confident grin and nod to the catcher gave the impression that he knew that he was about to become local folklore. Coach Hoover calmly turned his head and dispensed of some excess chewing tobacco juice. Before the spit hit the ground, Coach noticed that Bill was standing beside him on the first step of the dugout. To some, "Come In!" is a term used in positioning defensive fielders. To others, it means a quicker end to a really boring game.

# Chapter Two– Lessons Learned

## *My Basement's Leaking*

I am a proud, self-proclaimed nomad, always looking for fresh pasture. I can pack my essentials and be on the road in under five minutes. A relative once said that it's easy for me to be nomadic because I don't own anything. But in my eyes, I possess everything that any modern-day nomad could possibly need. A St. Croix 9 1/2 foot, 6-weight fly rod, a brand-new laptop, an automobile, and a GPS. Oh yeah, some clothing, and a few personal hygiene products. But while me and my Buick camel can easily travel to anywhere in a moment's notice, I do have a menagerie of memories stored in the basements of my happily-divorced parents. I've never watched the television shows "Hoarders" or "Intervention", but one of my family members just might, one day soon, nominate me to star on an upcoming episode of both.

Now remember, after reading this, that you'll think to yourself, "he couldn't have possibly made this stuff up." I didn't.

I gave away my Taiwanese, woman's boob-shaped, wooden massage tool and the replica Iranian battle axe and chain mail helmet. It certainly would've been silly to have things like that just lying around for no good reason. I only horde important crap, things worthy of precious storage space.

While looking for a hammer the other day, I stumbled upon my copy of an "acknowledgement of registration" from the Selective Service System. You never know, 35 years later, when your military draft status might come up during an employment interview. Along with this document, are the test results that revealed what career in which I might succeed. "You should consider 'Truck Driver'" *"Dammit, that's where I went wrong in life!"* Stupid restaurants. The results from my DAT test (Differential Aptitude Test) seem a little bit more on-target. Abstract Reasoning and Verbal Reasoning--in the 95 percentiles. Space Relations--30%. I can figure it out myself, just don't stand so close. That's how I read it.

In one box of treasures are my stuffed bears that I palled around with as a child. Smokey and Jo-Jo. Don't tell 'em if you see 'em, but they look worse-off than I do after all these years. Now the name "Smokey", I understand. Smokey the Bear. Belt, hat, badge, and everything. But Jo-Jo? Inspired by Jo-Jo White/ point guard for the Boston Celtics? He hadn't even been drafted into the NBA at this point. Who knows.

There are piles and piles of Valentine's Day cards from elementary school. There were no transgender cards available back then. Everyone gave everyone a card. *"Be my Valentine, signed Ralph"*. Not to be a homophobe there Ralph, but I've still got a leery eye on you, even after 45 years. As I matured, so did the cards. I kept stacks of letters and cards from the very first love of my life. And the second one. And a couple from a younger girl who kept promising me all sorts of immoral acts. Didn't really like her, but it made for good reading. And what a romantic little shit I was as a teenager. I wrote a poem for my first love that dreamed about living in a cave in Bolivia. *"Give me a blonde and a bottle of rum and everything will be all right".* Good try, but it didn't work.

For some reason, I have several of my Mother's grade school report cards. It was probably a leveraging/bartering tool on days that I brought home my own less-than-stellar grades from high school. A quick analysis of my college transcripts shows amazing success in chemistry and biology classes (thanks Mrs. Bauserman), but a total disinterest in elective courses such as 16th century music. Heck, in my defense, you had to WALK to the library to listen to the rockin' Hans Neusidler and his no-electric-guitar orchestra.

Grandfather Knode was a Free Mason. Thomas Jefferson, George Washington, and Grandad. Along with his embossed certificate of membership in the secretive District of Columbia chapter, I've kept forever his masonic apron and book of by-laws.

Grandmother Knode worked as a secretary for Senator Millard Tydings. A monogrammed wooden box that sat on his desk was given to her by the Senator as a sign of appreciation, after he left office in 1950. That wooden box now sits in my Mom's basement and contains a recipe typed by my Aunt B. The recipe is from Grandmother Knode for

"24-hour Salad", which is now a traditional dish served annually at our family's Thanksgiving Day meals.

Grandad Lambert worked during a period when a man's word and a hand-shake meant more than any written contract ever did. A receipt that I have, hand-written in the 1940's, was probably given to him as a monthly reminder by a local filling station; bagged ice and gasoline for the outrageous grand total of $3.10. Obvious price gouging. There are a few birthday cards from Grandad and Grandma Lambert. And several birthday cards from my Aunt Dot. On her way to family sainthood status, religiously every year, Aunt Dot would send birthday cards, each containing a five-dollar bill, to me, my two sisters and our 23 cousins. Each and every year, no matter where you were living. "How did she even know that I was in Savannah for three months this year?" Even if you didn't remember that it was your birthday, you did after you had checked your mailbox.

There's an issue of The Weekly World News, the now defunct, mostly fictional news tabloid publication which I always found so humorous. My live-in girlfriend at the time had out-nomad-ed me by moving out of our home while I was away at work. She later dropped off this edition as some sort of strange peace offering, knowing that I found the sarcasm very funny. "Redneck Aliens Takeover Trailer Park" The picture of a husband and wife, who had witnessed the invasion, was stoically captioned as saying "There goes the neighborhood". I think the giving of this gift had a double sarcastic message behind it. She was good at that.

Fishing was always a big part of my life and the basements are speckled with all sorts of fishing relics. A 40-year-old automatic fly reel that came mounted on my very first fly rod is still armed with the original fly line, forever cured with water from the Shenandoah. There's an antique wicker creel basket given to me by Neil Armstrong. Not the astronaut, silly. The UPS delivery driver who was a bar buddy of mine years ago, up at The Boston Beanery. His uncle had passed away and literally gave him the farm. Discovered out in the barn were three antique bamboo fly rods. *"Well Neil, those are all Montague rods, ya might want to check on their value."* A couple of weeks and a couple of thousands of dollars later, I received that creel basket as referral commission. Safely secured in a ceiling rack built by my Dad are another half dozen or so fly rods. Because, you know, you can never have too many fishing rods.

If your phone number was (xxx) 637-4293 and you're missing the rotary dial off your telephone, I have it. Give me a call.

I once was almost a father, but he died in womb. Tucked away in a box in the corner of the basement is a picture of Andrew, that was supposed to help with the grieving process. It doesn't work. The picture lies atop a couple of self-help books given as gifts, one of which is titled "The Expectant Father". Wish I had, but I never took the time to read those books.

My one younger sister had some serious home-sickness during her first summer camp experience. A letter that she had sent from camp, addressed to me and my other sister, was written on the second day at Camp Strawderman. The now empty letter once contained a single stick of chewing gum.

The letter read, "The gum is for Robin and Mary".

I wonder if I ever paid this parking ticket from Dulles airport. I had left my car unattended for two minutes near the airport's front doors, as I helped my Bulgarian buddy Lucy with her luggage, in a hurried attempt to catch her 6 A.M. flight back home. I guess that since I'm holding the ticket, that's not a good sign. Wasn't my car no how.

So, an ex-wife came yapping around my house one day, accusing me of possessing a set of fine china that we had received as a wedding present. I whole-heartedly denied any knowledge of the flowered pattern of plates and coffee cups, knowing dammed well the definition of a fifty/fifty split. She gets a hundred percent and I get zero. One afternoon, years later, I'm looking for something 'really' important in my small mountain of memorabilia, when I came across box after box stuffed with old newspapers. The Fredericksburg Free Lance-Star to be exact. Well, thanks funny, I used to live in Fredericksburg back when I was married. Whoops. I'd give that china set away for free, but it seems to make the food taste sour. (But a little revenge tastes sweet:) So in the basement it sits.

Before the days that OCD and ADD were invented, my childhood friend Stan and myself would spend hours playing with my electric football game. For the unknowledged, electric football sets were a small, metal playing field caused to vibrate by an electric motor, which created movement of the little, plastic figurines of football players. It was very loud and a lot of fun for a young boy. But being overly competitive, even at a young age, Stan and I took it to a whole new level of intensity. I have the spiral notebooks, filled with the plays and formations, that we hand-wrote and developed over time; we even kept detailed statistics of the games. The spiral notebooks, the still-functioning playing field and six plastic bags full of little players wearing their official NFL team colors, are resting comfortably in the basement, next to Coach Lee's new football playbook handouts that we received once a week before math class in my Senior year of high school.

There's the yellow lucky rabbit's foot that I wore on my Little League uniform's belt loop. Several engraved leather bracelets and a St. Christopher's necklace. A Happy Turkey Day card, the turkey picture created with the tiny, water-color stained left hand of my Goddaughter Rachel. An 8mm copy of "I am a Teenage Werewolf". I must have misplaced the one with Mr. Magoo.

Wait a minute, is that Zeppelin on the radio? Good Times, Bad Times...You know I had my share....

## *Left, Or Right?*

I was fishing down at the river one day when I heard a noise rustling in the bushes on the bank across the way. Maybe a deer? Maybe a very noisy squirrel? Another quick glance up from the river's waters and I saw a cute little dog sitting across the stream from me, contently watching me trying in vain to catch a fish. I went downstream and the dog mirrored my every move. Then he suddenly ran off back into the woods. It was soon time to go, so I headed back to my old pickup truck. And guess what. That same dog was sitting there by the truck waiting for me. He had no collar, no dog tag, and seemed to be lost. But he seemed very happy to see me. Some people in the backwoods of the area have this terrible habit of leaving dogs off in the woods when they can no longer be a good owner for whatever reason or if the dog is in its last days of life here on Earth. While I worried that he might be lost, I thought to myself that he Must live at a house nearby and comfortably reasoned with myself that he'd eventually find his way back home. After I loaded my fishing gear into the truck, I started on the trip back home. And there in the middle of the big road was that same little dog. So, I stopped without hesitation. I couldn't very well let him run around in the middle of the road like this, another vehicle might hit him. So, into my truck he went.

In contrast to his charming personality, he was a dirty and stinky dog. When we got to the house, I decided to give him an overdue bath. The fur on his rear-end was matted so badly with his own waste that I used scissors to slowly clip away the mess. This dog whom I had just met, shivered a bit in the tub's lukewarm water, but remained still and looked up at me with calm eyes, like he knew that I was doing a good thing.

And that dog was hungry. Very hungry. I had saved a ham bone from a family holiday dinner to use in making stock for a meal of my own. Well, plans they do change. I'm sure that I did feed him some other type of human doggie food, but all that I remember was the sight of him lying on his belly, chewing on a bone that was half his own body's length.

I didn't know the dog's name, so I called him Dirty Harry, because when I found him, he was 'dirty' and 'hairy'.

I couldn't keep Harry at my home for very long. It was a rental and dogs were not allowed.

So, Harry only stayed with me for two weeks. The bills don't pay themselves and I had to work. But what to do with the dog? Being a guy, I constructed a fence out of old wooden boards and chicken wire scraps, enclosing a section of the house's back deck. When I came home from work that first day, Harry was nowhere to be seen. I slowly peered over the edge of the deck, fearing that Harry may have taken a twenty foot, ill-advised leap of freedom. But after examining further evidence, it seemed that Harry had somehow scaled my homemade Wall of China. He was gone. I had lost a lost dog. How bad is that? Well dammit, I was determined that this story would have a happy storybook ending. So, I drove around for hours throughout the neighborhood, looking for any signs of my lost lost dog. That night, I slept with lights on so that the dog could easily see the house in the pitch black. But in the morning, there still was no Harry. I created "Lost Dog" flyers and posted them at the Post Office and the local grocery store, hoping that someone had seen him wandering about.

The next morning, a lady called and said that she had found Harry during the night. We planned to meet at the grocery store so that I could get my Harry back. Harry back, get it? As she drove into the parking lot, I could see Harry beaming excitement out of the rear passenger window, wearing one of those doggie smiles that says "I know that I screwed up, but you loves me anyways". But knowing that I couldn't keep Harry forever, I asked her if she knew of anyone that would like to have Harry as their very own. She looked at me with a puzzled expression on her face. *"My kids absolutely LOVE the dog…in fact, my son just asked me on the phone if the 'fluffy' dog was still there at our house"*. It only seemed right that Harry should go home with this wonderful family. So, I gave Harry to Cheryl and down the road they went.

Harry could have gone upstream instead of down, I could have let him wander there in the road and just headed back home alone.

Left or right. Make good choices and things just seem to work out for the best.

## *Devotion*

She was probably twenty years old. Five-foot, 9 inches tall with dirty brown, shoulder length hair. Her wheelchair was nothing special, pretty much run-of-the-mill as far as handicapped accessories go. It was 95 degrees outside this afternoon and she was wearing long pants. For a twenty-year-old, she wasn't making much of a fashion statement, but she was sporting some pretty cool-looking Nike's.

So, I'm sitting there with my Dad in the eye doctor's waiting room. It's quite the good gig those optometrists have, lines of patients waiting their turn to have their vision improved. Most of the patients were of Social Security Benefits age, which means that they had old, worn-out eyes and good insurance coverage. There were a few middle-aged folks dressed in failed attempts to mask the years, but just this one young woman that actually appeared to be young. We had arrived an hour early for my Dad's scheduled appointment, so there was a lot of time to kill. I dove into the pile of magazines on the table; Virginia Living, Newsweek, Time, and lots of travel magazines pushing trips to places that I could only hope to visit. Dad was finally called and began his journey through the various livestock gates of "Welcome/Check-In", "You think You're Checked-In" "You're almost Checked-In" and finally "The Examination Room". I started to get bored and my gimpy knee was aching, so I went for a short walk outside.

When I returned to the waiting room, progress had thankfully been made. Almost all of those who had been waiting were no longer there. Except for this young woman and her Mother. A secretive glance or three in their direction quickly brought me to two conclusions.

First off, the younger woman's afflictions were permanent. She had obvious disabilities, both learning and physical. The wheelchair wasn't going to be a temporary home.

Secondly, somewhere there's a portrait entitled "A Mother" and I was looking right at the painting's subject as she sat directly across the room from me. She wasn't embarrassed by her daughter. She didn't tell her to 'hush' or take her out to the parking lot. When the Daughter laughed a silly laugh at something that she herself had said, and in which only she could find the real humor, the Mother would smile a warm smile and gently rub her Daughter's shoulder. The younger woman wasn't a cheerleader or a valedictorian. She was her Mother's Daughter.

I'm flipping through a special edition of Time magazine that highlighted athlete after athlete, all members of this year's U.S. Olympic Team. The biggest. The fastest. The most agile. The Gold Medal favorites. And then this young woman in a wheelchair begins to sing.

> Jesus loves me this I know
>
> For the Bible tells me so
>
> Little ones to him belong
>
> They are weak but he is strong

She sang the entire hymn, word for meaningful word. The Mother never looked up from the magazine that she was reading, but smiled such a beautiful smile as her Daughter proudly finished her rendition of the children's favorite. *"That was nice"* the Mother said to her Daughter.

> Them eye doctors sure are something.
>
> I took my Dad in for a check-up
>
> and I came out with clearer vision.

## *Doing Laundry for Some Reason*

No matter what your belief during those moments where a certain force seems to come into play and affect the outcome of a situation, you've got to admit that there's been a time or two where you've stopped and thought to yourself "That was unbelievable". Be it coincidence, destiny, or Divine intervention from a Heavenly Spirit, there just has to be something that factors into the end result at unexplained moments.

In the small town where I lived, there were two laundromats open to the public and zero facilities in my apartment. Being a typical, single male, I did my laundry every week or two, or whenever the dirty clothes on the floor became annoying. The one laundromat in town was newer, but seemed to always be frequented by a shadier, louder crowd. With children. So, I went to the 'old reliable'. This laundromat was always quiet, probably because the poor quality of equipment sent everyone else across town to the other. I would do a crossword puzzle while waiting, plus, on this day, I needed to fax my resume off to a potential new employer and the motel next door had a fax machine that I could pay to use.

On the walk back from the motel, a car slowed beside me as its passenger window rolled down. It was my best friend Mitch.

*"Whatcha doing, Snapper Head?"*

*"Just sent a resume to that company that I was telling you about.*

*And doing some laundry"*

*"Me too! Hop in"*

It was only 400 yards back to the laundromat. Mitch had been on a laundry-beer-run after starting his first load of dirty clothes. The lighthearted chit-chat suddenly took a U-turn.

*"Fred died last night"*

His Father had been sick and hospitalized for some time, so it came as no surprise. Along with his vigilant family at bedside, Mitch had played some of his Father's favorite music on a little boom box, some Johnny Horton I believe, as his Father left this Earth forever.

We cracked open a beer each and spent the next hour and a half talking about his Dad, memories of Life with him, and just telling old stories.

Fred was a big man, both in height and command presence. During the spin cycle, we laughed about the night that our friend Jay and myself had spent the night at Mitch's house, on Halloween of all evenings. As twelve-year-olds, we were certain that Ricky Wilkins and the older boys in the neighborhood would be out later, terrorizing the neighbors with rolls of toilet paper and bars of soap. And WE were going to catch them in the act. Clad in only underwear, we headed out into the darkness, the backyard grass cold with an early dew. It was just before midnight as we began our patrol.

A crack of a tree limb froze us in our tracks like startled deer and we took a Three Stooges pose as we peeked around the corner of the house. A thunderous voice then bellowed from above our heads.

*"WHAT are you boys doin'? Get BACK in the HOUSE!"*

We scurried back into the den, scared silly with giggles as we crawled back into our sleeping bags.

The stories continued. Mitch had walked in his sleep one night right into Fred's bedroom, thinking it was the bathroom, after going right instead of left. Fred woke and stopped him, just as Mitch lifted the toilet lid pant leg of Fred's business suit draped over an upholstered chair.

Slingshots. Car stereos. Ex-wives. The order of the stories told was random, but perfectly in place.

I could always understand why Mitch had been doing laundry that day, just twelve hours after his Father had died. The world was spinning all around his head and he needed an escape for a minute.

But why had we run into each other that day? A random place, at a random time, doing a random chore. No one else had come into the laundromat during our entire hour and a half talk about life. Just two friends, sitting there drinking a beer, talking about things. After the dryer buzzed at the end of its cycle, the last of the clean laundry was folded, and we went back to our separate worlds. But closer together.

## *Death of a Mentor*

Mr. Renggli's obituary was in the Herald yesterday. After hearing the news, my sister and I were going down memory lane and I started into my long list of Hamilton Restaurant stories...kindda made me smile. This was my first real job in life. And quite the learning experience that it was.

The dreaded "Walk of Doom" ... was taking a gentleman's steak back to the kitchen because it 'ain't well-done enough'. I'd shiver from the fear of repercussions as I put the NY Strip, slathered in ketchup, back under the heat lamp and calmly explain "Uh, he'd like this cooked a little more.

*"Damn peasants!!!!!!!!!!!!"* When food orders were complete in the window, he'd slam his 10-inch chef knife on the little 'come get it' metal bell and holler *"Dammit Betsy, Pick Up, Pick Up!!!"* There was a Betsy, but sometimes that's what he'd call little teenage-me, just to keep me in my place.

Health inspectors had never worked around the world as he had and he saw them as an inferior form of life. Yet with amazing charm and grace, he'd walk, talk, and listen to them during inspections, and then, as expected, curse them after they had departed, a 1/2-inch ash hanging from his Benson & Hedges cigarette.

One Friday evening, I was working alongside fellow servers Betsy and Anna Mae. Forty-five-year-old twin sisters, whose combined height was about nine feet, seven inches tall. They probably got aggravated at amusement parks. During the heat of the work chaos, Betsy asked me to reach an upper shelf in the storage room. The ancient stainless steel hot table wasn't exactly smooth. A jagged edge caught the seam of my khaki slacks and they tore from belt loop to knee. I'm standing in the middle of the kitchen, showing bloomers and bare leg to everyone. Chaos came to a temporary halt and everyone laughed. Everyone except Mr. Renggli. His step-son had stopped-by on his way home from the dry cleaners. He and I were the same size and miraculously he had a matching pair of khakis in his car. Into the walk-in refrigerator, I went. As I lowered my pants to my ankles, I came face to leaf with a large container of freshly prepped salad mix. I'll never look at lettuce the same way again, guaranteed. I returned to my seven tables without missing a single step. *"And how's your dinner...enjoy the rest of your meal"*

And there were the mornings after a long night of partying at the Edinburg Mill; I'd be on my way to work, thinking that it would obviously be much easier to drive my car into the ditch as compared to working eight stressed-filled hours waiting tables. I'd get there at 6:15 AM and find him in the back-kitchen area. Coffee and cigarette in hand, calmly reading the morning newspaper, he'd already have made a batch of buttermilk biscuits. Between 6:30 and 9:30, he and I would serve up to 150 people for breakfast...he cooked, I served. By 9:30, my BAC would be down to around .17 and I was starting to feel better about the day. I think that I'll take a break and finish my 6:15 AM cup of coffee. I'd looked around and he'd already have homemade bread going into the oven, the steam-table set up for lunch, and would be prepping the two noon specials (i.e. 2 pieces of hand breaded fried chicken, 2 vegetables and a homemade roll, $2.65 not including a beverage or tax. The regulars squawked when it went up to $2.75). Lessons in organization that I learned from him, which years later, would make me stop occasionally and think "Mr. Renggli". I always took pride in the fact that he'd leave me alone in the restaurant some afternoons and 'go to the bank'. This meant he'd go to the bank and then head home to walk his dogs. A privilege he never entrusted in the waitresses, not even Dot, the restaurant's living artifact. When I first came home from college for Christmas vacation, I called him to see if he needed any help over the holidays. He responded matter of factly, in his blunt Swiss/German accent, *"Yes, put on a nice shirt and pants. You can wait tables"*. I had only cooked up until this point. During that first week of waiting tables, there was a fairly significant snow storm. One afternoon, he instructed me to take a to-go order over to room 33 of the motel. That's when I first met Mrs. Gesundburg, an eccentric, large, older woman who was dressed in a sheer nightgown when she invited me into her motel room. When I returned to the restaurant through the kitchen back door, there was Mr. Renggli, cigarette dangling from his mouth, reading the newspaper at the back-prep table. He never looked up. But he had the biggest grin on his face and was chuckling to himself. He had known her for years as a regular guest of the motel and had set me up for embarrassment's sake.

Mr. Renggli worked in his restaurant every day, 6 in the morning till 10 at night. He cooked every meal himself, with a little help on Friday and Saturday evenings. The food served was consistently very good. Not the norm among the small list of restaurants in our area. Traveling guests of the motel would never believe me when I said that the fresh flounder was fresh (I had cleaned it out back of the restaurant that afternoon). People drove from DC just to get a pint of his homemade Bleu cheese dressing, and then of course, stay for dinner. I'd work five days in a week's time and would start my day off at the Hamilton with a cup of peanut soup and a club sandwich (four slices of bread, not three).

During my last Christmas at the Hamilton, all the employees (all 7 or 8) received presents. The very long-term employees, Dot, Betsy, and Anna Mae, received some very nice things...clothes, gift certificates and the like. I called Mr. Renggli "Chief", coincidentally the same moniker that I used with my own father. In a strange arrangement, which I never fully understood, Chief and his ex-wife had 'a joint custody' of the restaurant. She was always around. The ex-wife and her new husband gave me some beer and blocks of cheese as a Christmas gift. Mr. Renggli gave me a beautiful electric blanket. He'd scream at me, curse at me and he knew that I lived in an overly ventilated, wood stove-heated cabin. While we opened presents in the dining room, he never came out of the kitchen. But he knew that I knew what he knew.

Dammit heaven, HOT STUFF, COMING OVER!!!

Joseph Andreas Renggli, 79, of Woodstock, died suddenly at his home on July 22, 2005.

Mr. Renggli was born and raised in Lucerne, Switzerland. After graduating from school, he attended Palace Hotel School. He had traveled to many countries in his early career as a culinary chef, always learning to speak their language. He spoke seven languages. He came to the United States from Jamaica, where he was chef at Tower Isle. Later, he owned and operated the Hamilton Restaurant in Woodstock for many years.

## The Talent Show

Just like a lot of other people, I ingest news daily, from every possible media source. Internet, television, newspaper, and radio. The 'paper' selling headlines are filled with death, destruction, and unthinkable crimes. The race for political office, millions of illegal aliens, mass murder, ACLU this, ACLU that.

Tonight, I went to an elementary school talent show. I'm not going to tell you the exact location of the school...just in case you work for the ACLU. I showered and shaved beforehand and wore a nicer pair of shorts for the big night out on the town. As I got out of my car and walked towards the school, I began to question my own personal hygiene checklist. But then it dawned on me that the odor was, in fact, recently spread chicken manure on a nearby field and not my normal bathing habits.

The gymnasium was packed. Fortunately, I had connections that had saved me a seat--- front and center. Tickets for free elementary school talent shows are not easy by which to come, so I had to pull a few strings.

Much to my surprise, the talent show began with what was described as a 'very abbreviated PTO meeting'. As usual, at the beginning of any big moment, I was a little bit confused. I was looking around for Jim and Tammy...and their manager, band director, MC guy with the perfect, man-bouffant, naturally grey hair. OH, P.T.O. Well if I seemed surprised that it was a parent-teacher meeting instead of an evangelical television show, then they appeared equally surprised when I proposed two new amendments to the constitution of their organization. Not knowing me or my parent -teacher intentions, both proposals were instantly shot down.

The director of the program instructed us to 'join together in the Pledge of Allegiance'. Faces turned towards the American flag hanging on the gymnasium wall, men took off their hats, 350 hands were placed over a heart and all the voices spoke as one. I cannot, ever, at this point, help but think of all that we have which is so good, those who have fallen so that we can enjoy these benefits, and how good it is to be an American citizen.

The talent show began. It went on f.o.r.e.v.e.r... which is a good thing. You could pick out the kids who had been in the 'spotlight' before. The others will just be that much better with practice. Even if a kid sucked, their friends cheered them on, their teachers congratulated them, and their parents loved them. And they will be better-off the next time that they try doing something VERY scary. The acts consisted of singing, dancing, the playing of musical instruments and a few comedy skits.

There was the tiny first grader, dressed as a cat, doing her wonderful little cat dance. Another small girl, who apparently specialized in Olympic-style rhythmic dance, kept dropping her streamer and balloon, but continued bouncing around in her tutu like no one was watching. An older girl sang "Amazing Grace" a Capella. There were at least five religious based songs performed this evening, but no one protested. And it seemed that no one but myself even had the thought of a protest pop into their mind.

There was an inconsistent flow of acts coming to the stage, but a constant flow of adults coming forward, all wearing big smiles, and carrying cameras and camcorders to record the talent for all of eternity.

An earlier announcement in the evening was made to let everyone know that the bake sale in the lobby was to benefit Mr.& Mrs. So & So.... the announcer explaining *"well, I think that everyone knows the reason"*. Everyone scurried to the bake sale during the long-anticipated intermission. I felt like the only one who didn't know 'Why', but I joined in line.

(Upcoming American Idol reference, which I never watch) Simon, the black man, and the Latin chick voted my niece and nephew as the greatest performers of the evening. Well... maybe that was just my own biased voting. But if those three judges had been there, they'd have been treated with grace, dignity, and about forty-two other wonderful qualities that are found every day in the Shenandoah Valley.

## *On Mother's Day*

One afternoon at my restaurant in Fredericksburg, we were enjoying a booming bit of business from the highly predictable Mother's Day crowd. At 1:30 in the afternoon, the churches had all emptied and a small mass of humanity had joined us to enjoy a meal and more importantly, demonstrate through a dining experience how special their Moms were to them.

It was a great atmosphere, 200 happy folks chatting and smiling between bites. Even the 75 or so waiting at the front door appeared happy, enjoying time with family, not stressed over having to wait for their turn at lunch. There was a pep in the step of the wait staff army, somehow smiling as they kept pace with the crowd.

The screams of a young child shattered that comfortable atmosphere. I headed in the direction of the ear-piercing noise.

A young girl had lodged her foot between the decorative brass handrail post and the first step leading down from the back-dining room. Her ten-year-old sister was trying to calm her down, but with very little success. I knelt in front of the little girl in a worthless show of support. The older sister patted her sister on the shoulder and said *"Amy, it's O.K., I'll get Mom"*. And off she went, leaving me holding the hand of a bawling little girl, center stage in the big ring of a bustling circus.

The girl was dressed in her Sunday best, looked like a living porcelain doll, her big, brown doe eyes producing a river of tears that flowed down her little cheeks.

And then a strange calm came across her face. The crying stopped and the tears were no more. A tinkling of urine began splashing across the floor's mosaic tiles and the toes of my Rockport shoes. Suddenly, in a poof like a superhero, Mom arrived and whisked her daughter away from danger, the girl's foot magically released from its painful predicament.

Because that's what Mothers do.

I grabbed a mop and proceeded to clean up a pool of pee. Because that's what restaurant managers do. (wink...wink)

To everyone's first hero, Happy Mother's Day.

## *Walnut Street*

The morning's commute led from Spring Street to Main. A last-second detour found neighborhoods not traveled in years. The old home of a childhood friend. Abandoned houses. This side street seems to have become the town's first 'slum', with seventy-year-old buildings and out of business signs. Everything looks dirty. The little road winds to the right and over the railroad tracks. No one seems to use turn signals anymore; the annoying ding of the blinker sounds as an intersection's stop sign lies ahead. Across Walnut Street, on the right curb's corner painted yellow, sits a young man. His hands cover his face like he's rubbing tired eyes, but he continues to rest his face in the palms. His body occasionally convulses from sobbing, but not with screams or cries of sadness, his body twitches from holding it all in. Another young man, visually older looking than the first, walks towards the tears and puts a sympathetic hand on the grief-stricken shoulder. They appear to be house painters or roofers, dressed in dirty jeans and work boots and not the types to be crying or comforting.

The blue minivan finally creeps by, allowing for a left-hand turn. But before the approaching stoplight, only two hundred yards away, numerous scenarios are processed by the brain. Did he discover a dead person at the house? A relative? A friend? Did he receive a life-changing phone call? It couldn't be work-related because nothing on the job would be that important.

Oh, wipe away the thoughts of a scene of suicide. By gun or by rope, it makes the conscience shutter, especially if it had indeed been a loved one involved.

Dinner with the Parents tonight may be over-cooked or cold and will probably consist of the same old-same old. But the meal will be wonderful. The conversation may be confusing or may not contain a single spoken word. But it will be heartwarming.

Tomorrow's newspaper will let the world know for just a moment if someone had died on Walnut Street.

## *Why We Play Games*

The backyard on Susan Avenue was completely dark by 8 PM, only the shadows of trees standing still and young boys running wild could be sensed by the naked eye.

Across the road and a million miles away, was the glow of the high school football field, a full-blown production occupying the rest of the entire Earth. The teams across the street had uniforms of blue and gold and red and white. Steel tipped cleats and 200 pound athletes made quite the rumble at the snap of each new play. The cheerleaders cheered, synchronized with the beat of the marching band's drums. Parents proudly reacted after every snap of the ball, with various expressions of cheers and jeers. Some young girls looked on with starry eyes, while others giggled in secret conversations held in small huddles.

The backyard teams on Susan Avenue weren't quite as uniformed. Plaid, long-sleeved shirts, or bulky sweatshirts topped off the dirty blue jeans and once-white tennis shoes. The leaders of the opposing sides barked out plays to their teammates as they hand wrote the X's and O's with dirty fingers onto the palms of their hands. The leaders might not have been the most athletic members of the bunch, but they did naturally what they did best. Strategies were drawn around the abilities of the bigger or faster or more gifted young men. The ones who possessed neither fast lips or fast legs settled into their roles as blockers or rushers, the positions less glorious but equally as important to the success of the team.

Whether it's sports or music or fashion, there will always be iconic 'Stars' that young people look up to and idolize.

Down in the basement, safely stored in boxes full of memorabilia, are autographed black & white pictures of Johnny Unitas, Bart Starr, John Mackey, and Sonny Jurgensen. Before the days of the computer age, a young fan could mail in a request to the NFL team of your Idol and they would mail back an 8 X 10 glossy, signed by the football Greats themselves.

During the early 1970's, Julius Erving was an emerging basketball superstar, first playing in the ABA with the Virginia Squires and then a perennial All-Star in the NBA. "Dr. J" was a human highlight reel, the likes of which little boys like me had never seen before. I first became enchanted with "The Doctor" while watching him operate on the grainy tube of our family's little black and white television. The low-quality display couldn't damper the electricity of his high-flying artistry, fans rose to their feet every time that he touched the ball and collectively held their breath as he drove to the basket. He walked the walk without the talk and gained respect from the masses, not from being flashy, but by being a hardworking teammate, a leader by example. Of course, it didn't hurt that he could leap and touch the top of the backboard and grip a basketball like a grapefruit, like me with my Nerf ball as I pretended to be him. I'd watch the tail end of the morning news every day before school, for weeks at a time, in the off chance that they'd show a clip of "The Doc" in action.

The adults that teach the budding young athletes the basics of the sports that we play are doing it for a variety of reasons. Some are 'giving back' out of respect to those that had coached them in the past. Some coach as a genuine civic duty while others are just adding a notch to a self-important belt of social status. And many a parent/coach has learned something brand new, like the game of soccer, so they can be a support alongside their own child who was in pursuit of a character building, healthy activity.

Kids, of course, see things differently. Literally, as a small person, looking up to an adult who's in charge of the activity. And figuratively, as a young person, looking up to an adult for guidance and knowledge.

It's bothersome to me, for some reason, the way some children lack respect for their elders nowadays. Part of the underlying cause is the fault of the adults themselves, with the whole "everyone gets a ribbon just for participating" mentality. The coach's name is not "Bob", it's Mr. Danley. He is not your new best friend. He is older and wiser, and is a figure of authority to whom you should listen and learn from.

I played a lot of games of sport in my younger days and I had a lot of different coaches from whom I learned. I could go on and on about the different styles and personalities, but that will have to wait for a different day. But if I was playing a game of 'word association' and I was presented with the word 'Coach', I'd instantly respond-"Walters".

When I was a kid, my family lived a block from the town park. I used to run through the neighbors' lawns every morning to shoot hoops for an hour or two at the park. Afternoons were spent playing tennis, because there were usually cute girls involved. At night, I'd run back over to the park after dinner and join pick-up games of basketball until it got too dark to see. Rainy days would find me alone in the family's basement, doing countless ball-handling drills, imitating Pete Maravich, except for the floppy socks. In seventh grade, our High School's Boys' Basketball team was playing in the district championship, in a town far away. I listened intently to the play-by-play on the radio in my parent's bedroom, and felt real despair when they lost. Our High School was comprised of Grades 8-12 when I tried out and made the 8th grade team, my first exposure to organized basketball. Students got free admission to the school's sporting events and we'd fill the stands and scream our lungs out as high-flying Stevie Jackson was soaring above the rims

63

and center Rocky Dinges had epic battles against All-District Harry Jordan from Rappahannock County. In 9th grade, now on the JV team, I got the chance to scrimmage against our Varsity team. It was then that I got my first introduction to Coach Walters.

Coach Walters is a legend at our High School. He coached our teams to over 500 victories during his career. He is in the Virginia High School League - Book of Records' list of all-time winningest coaches. He prowled the sidelines like Indiana's legendary Bobby Knight, except there'd be moments of smiles and laughs between the intense flares and growls. Coach could somehow scream right up in your face while delivering his message with his pointed finger without ever touching your nose.

After our team got scorched for 10 points in the 1st quarter by Strasburg's All-District point guard, I received the old, inspirational *"IF HE GOES TO TAKE A PISS, I WANT YOU IN THE BATHROOM WAITIN' FOR HIM!"* (along with other words of encouragement). I was hyper-ventilating as I waited directly in front of their time-out huddle, like a two-legged Jaguar waiting for an unsuspecting antelope. His jersey Number was 10. I can remember that after all these years and now hate the color purple because my face was planted on the front of his jersey for 24 more minutes that night and 100's more over the next 2 years.

Actual games were easy because practices were intense. There were countless wind sprints and 'whistle-less' loose ball drills, bloody noses, and wood-burned knees. We pushed ourselves because Coach believed in us, encouraged us, and expected us to succeed. We learned the value of working as a team, working strategically together and ultimately learned that hard work does pay off. I can proudly say that each of my 3 years on the Varsity team were winning seasons. We were taught the how's and why's of the skills needed to win, counseled when we fell short of our abilities and praised when we succeeded.

The simple definition of 'Coach' is someone who teaches and trains an athlete or performer, but Merriam left off the important part 'that will last a lifetime'.

In my many years of managing restaurants, I've interviewed 1000's of potential new employees. Their stories and work experiences ran the predictable gamut from desperate now to restaurant 'lifers'. But every once in a while, you'd sit across the table from a young person, nervously holding an application with a blank work-history, while at the same time giving off an air of confidence.

"No Sir, this would be my very first job."

"I have always enjoyed being a part of a team"

"Yes Sir, nothing like getting that 'W', especially against a team that was supposed to be better than you".

Well, Mr. Winner, sorry that you didn't receive any pretty ribbons at the swim meet. You start Monday.

It was a busy Friday night at the steak house with dozens of hungry patrons waiting at the front door for their chance at a table. As I scurried to the front desk to check with the host staff, my head was spun by the sound of a voice that I had not heard in 25 years.

"HEY, LAMBERT!"

Like a 16-year-old hoopster heading to the bench to learn of a change in defensive strategy, I bee-lined it over to Table 601 and a smiling Coach Walters and his wife.

"I sure could use a good point guard this year"

Well, almost all things are possible.

## *My Aunt B*

You know that "Christmas morning feeling" that you got as a kid, on a Tuesday afternoon in July when a package arrived from your Aunt, postmarked with something about Bangkok and something about the U.S. Army. Well, probably not. But I do.

On my Father's side of my family, I have numerous aunts and uncles, which in turn gave me dozens of cousins, who themselves now have dozens of their own children. Hard working, down-to-earth type folks; sort of reminds you of "The Walton's". My Mom has one sister. My Aunt B.

She never had any children of her own. She's a lot like me (or more accurately, I'm a lot like her); Those little yard-ape, ankles-biters sure are cute and all, but they're an enormous responsibility. It's a lot more convenient to live vicariously through other people's children. You just entertain the little snot-noses for a short while. Gain their temporary trust by teaching 'em a few harmless bits of information that their parents would never dare speak (i.e. Texas Hold-'em Poker; it's good for the math skills, learning the art of straight-faced lying and developing money management skills). Hand-crank the key on the middle of their little backs until the spring is wound tight. Feed 'em a soda and a pound of candy.

Then, when they're just beginning to spasm, quickly give them back to their parents. *"Have a nice evening!"*

Andy Griffith's Aunt Bee was nothing like my Aunt B. The matriarch of Mayberry had a quiet, reserved personality. She was always fixin' up fried chicken for Andy and Opie or baking pies for a local community event. She wore drab clothing and sang in the church choir each Sunday. *"Don't be late for suppa!"*

Aunt B is the only person that I've ever known to own an 8mm camera. And thank goodness that she did. Not everyone my age has home videos documenting their childhood years. An 8mm camera was something unique to the world during that period of time. Unique, exciting, evolving, interesting, trend-setting. And she also owned one of those cameras.

Her movies still exist, preserved forever in a digital format. The shaky, grainy, black and white film cells capture images of everyday life as it appeared in our small town during the late 1950's and early 60's. Bulky Plymouths cruising down Main Street. Me and my knees taking a bath in the kitchen sink. The local volunteer fire department putting out a practice blaze on a small farm pond. The family dog. Snow. And lots of family gatherings. As the camera scans, slowly around the living room, men in white shirts and suspenders recline in high-back chairs, some smoking pipes or cigarettes while solving the world's problems. The ladies huddle in groups confined to the shadowy corners, somehow secondary, as was the custom of the times. Polite children stare dumbstruck at the camera as proud parents look on. Lots of black rimmed glasses and bouffant hairdo's. Those film clips appear to the viewer as a slow-moving portrait come to life. Of course, there was me, the OCD, Ritalin-deprived, poster child for hyperactivity bouncing off assorted furniture, while juggling family heirlooms. But then there was Aunt B. In her physical prime, Aunt B was a 'looker'. A cross between a silly Audrey Hepburn and a subdued Lucille Ball. She would bat her eye-lashes and flash a smile for the camera, then strut off into the distance like a runway model, only to morph into a 'flapper' doing the Charleston, look back over her shoulder and giggle uncontrollably. The living, slow moving portraitlike film was shot in black and white, but flashes of color seemed to appear whenever she crashed the scene.

In a way, Aunt B followed her Mother's footsteps into the working world. My Grandmother worked as a private secretary for U.S. Senator Millard Tydings in our Nation's capital (i.e. Tydings Committee vs. Joseph MacCarthy). Aunt

B.'s path led her outside of the Washington, D.C. area. She worked various positions, but primarily at U.S. installations and embassies around the world. Along the way, she met my Uncle Bob. Uncle Bob would eventually become a 30-year veteran of our armed forces, serving in 4 of the 5 military branches during his career. They married and spent many years of bliss together during their world-wide tour, eventually 'retiring' in Las Vegas, Nevada. Retiring meant Aunt B arranging junket packages for high stake gamblers at the Riviera Hotel and Casino. Uncle Bob becoming the head of security for Vegas Village Shopping centers.

The packages that arrived at our house when I was young came from places that I only knew about by reading a globe or a newspaper. Berlin, Germany. Bangkok, Thailand. Tehran, Iran. My gifts included a green Lederhosen-type outfit. A wooden massage tool shaped like a set of woman's breasts. A hand-carved wooden cow bell (clacker). A bag of matchbooks from everywhere. A large wooden elephant. A Knights-of-Arabia looking replica metal shield, helmet, and battle ax. A gold puzzle ring set with my Garnet birthstone. Souvenir travel patches from Alsace, Nederland, and Ankara.

The Fiat that I drove in high school came by cargo ship from Europe when Aunt B's next move wouldn't allow a vehicle. The cuckoo clock hanging in our dining room came from Germany's Black Forest. It drove our family crazy. May have had something to do with me constantly setting the hands of the clock forward so I could watch that little bird do his thing.

Between the National Geographic Magazine and The Travels of Aunt B, I developed the itch to go somewhere/anywhere at a very young age. Three days after I graduated from high school, I hopped on a plane and visited Aunt B. in Las Vegas for the summer. There WAS a world outside of Woodstock, Virginia! Just before my 21st birthday, I went back a second time and stayed for a year and a half.

Aunt B is now in the prime of her life, just recently celebrating her 78th birthday. She is legally blind because of macular degeneration. She has suffered from narcolepsy since she was a young teenager. Her bouffant hairdo has been traded in on a fine selection of wigs. Her shapely gams are not quite as shapely or sturdy anymore.

What brought Aunt B. here to now live in Virginia is not a happy story by any means. It was common for her and Uncle Bob to vacation separately. And during vacation time, there was limited contact between the two of them, especially before the age of cell phones. It was just a practice that helped them keep the marriage a happy one, like not going to bed mad at one another. A few years ago, Aunt B flew in from Las Vegas to spend a couple of weeks visiting with my Mom here in Virginia. During the week before her return trip, there were no panicky phones calls to remind Uncle Bob when and where to pick her up. He knew the time, date, and number of her return flight. They had gone through the routine dozens of times before. When she arrived at MacCarran International Airport, Uncle Bob was not there to greet her. Aunt B, narcoleptic and legally blind, sat in a waiting lounge for four hours, but still no sign of Uncle Bob. She then called friends for a ride home and then called police to break into her house. Uncle Bob had a fatal heart attack while taking a shower. Counting the newspapers in the driveway, it seemed that he had been under running water for several days. The image of my little Aunt sitting in that big airport, waiting patiently for the man that she had loved for years, as he lay dead in a tub at their home...it just makes me very sad. Like tears-sad.

Aunt B.'s house here in Woodstock is just minutes from my home. It's a nice little two-bedroom duplex located in a quiet neighborhood filled with retirees such as herself. But unlike the 'old folks' homes of her neighbors, her home is that one museum which you really enjoyed visiting. Hanging in the hallway are the autographs given to her by the Apollo 11 astronauts, while they toured Berlin after their big flight. An autographed card that reads "Best Wishes, Richard M. Nixon". A Vietnam War aircraft carrier picture, with various airmen's handwritten notes thanking Uncle Bob for his leadership and wishing him well in his next assignment. There's a framed poster promoting a bull fight in Mexico that Aunt B. had attended. Another poster is an advertisement for a ballet in Paris. The beautiful artwork depicts the prima ballerina for the evening's show, who just happens to be my second-cousin Helen. In the living room, there are table lamps constructed out of antique brass hookah pipes. When you're almost tired of asking 'what is that? or who is that?', you walk into the den. A look at the walls covered with pictures of Vegas entertainers and you find yourself asking

*"You met Wayne Newton?"*

I spent most of my life preparing food for people. As in professionally. People paid for the little nuggets of goodness. Nowadays, I'll spend an afternoon creating something yummy just for the pure enjoyment of cooking, which might sound odd to some folks. Aunt B would be one of those who would question the phrase "enjoyment of cooking". The last thing that she seared was the inside of her microwave oven while trying to burn a frozen dinner. I'll deliver dinner or dessert to her front door, announcing my arrival as *"Meals on Wheels!"* Every tenth or eleventh meal will get a panned review such as *"I just couldn't eat it. I threw the second chop in the trash"*. *"Well, what'd you want me to do, lie to ya?"*. Aunt B would be the one in the group to bluntly ask *"That's what you're wearing to dinner?"* Yet I continue my pilgrimage of delivered meals. She cracks me up with her bluntness and flamboyant natural self. Aunt Bee of Mayberry was known around town as simply Aunt Bee. Friends and acquaintances of mine will ask *"How is your Aunt B?"* They don't know her first, last or maiden name, but they remember the person. She wears fake bunny ears at Easter and reindeer antlers at Christmas. She loves a glass of blush before dinner. She tells the same stories of her younger days over and over and over, each time with a different twist or untruth, but always with enthusiasm, grace, wit, and color. Just like her starring role in those old home movies of hers. Nowadays, she'll bitch about this and that, but who could really blame her. Her husband's a memory. Old friends and family are leaving this world at an increasing pace. The eyesight's almost gone and the body doesn't work as well as it once did. Images might find it difficult to enter her eyes, but twinkles still find their way out. When she wakes from a narcoleptic session, it's with a smile or giggle, like to say *"Yep, I'm back."*

As Aunt B skipped around the world, she was often asked as to where she was from. Her own little running joke was to answer (in a heavy Southern drawl) *"I'm from Pugh's Run, Virginia"*. (Pugh's Run isn't even really a place, but a small stream just north of Woodstock). When Aunt B came back to Virginia to live for good, family members met her at the airport. Like hired limo drivers, we stood stoically near the departure gate and held up our own little homemade sign. You got your signs for Thompson, Smith, and Jones. Our little sign simply read "Pugh's Run".

A lot of gifts from Aunt B showed up at our front door. The common thread amongst them was a reason to dream. The world's a great big adventure.

## *1000 Words about a Woman*

The first time that I met Ms. Gesundburg was on an unexpected blind date. I was blind to the fact that she was going to be my date that morning. In the early hours of a pretty significant snowstorm, my boss had instructed me, while wearing a totally straight-face, to deliver a special food order over to Room 33 of the adjoining motel. I strutted myself across the snow-covered parking lot, awkwardly wearing my waiter's uniform which was topped with a vest and bow tie, happily free from the restaurant, if only for a moment. I politely knocked on the door and waited patiently in the cold. Suddenly, the door swung open as the winds again began to howl, kicking up a fog of fine snow.

And there she stood.

"Come on In, Honey!"

Probably in her sixties, she stood near six feet tall and was big boned, as they say. She was barefoot and wearing a flowing, sheer nightgown. My first thought was one of fear. The fear of how embarrassing it will be for my family and friends after I was discovered suffocated to death while unwillingly losing my virginity to a much older woman in a motel room. But fortunately, that never happened, my male ego and emotional growth still free of scars.

The adage "You can't judge a book by its cover" was so true when it came to Mrs. Gesundburg. With her dramatic, grand entrances through the restaurant's front door, she was probably assumed by traveling diners as being a bag-woman who had lost her way. She was verbally as loud as the outfits that she wore, bright mismatched floral patterns of clothing, wearing flipflops topped with plastic flowers and big sunglasses stuck in a mass of unkempt, fly-away blonde hair.

A large Phyllis Diller. She addressed each and every person on the way to her favorite table as if they were an old friend, the tone of her voice always positive and happy as it broke the normal ho-hum of the dining room and bounced around its walls. It's not that she had a 'voice that would carry', she just talked loud.

It was rumored that she had a habit of marrying wealthy men, each of whom then died under suspicious circumstances. One of the dearly departed had owned large tracts of land near our nation's capital, which were later sold to become what is now one of the largest shopping complexes near the city. Another of the Unfortunates died owning countless shares of stock in Ma Bell before the conglomerate's breakup. She may have had periods of mourning, but she wasn't hurtin'. She owned a house not a 1/2 mile from the hotel, but during periods of extreme inclement weather like this storied day, she'd simply rent a room at the motel, supplying herself with everything that a girl could need. A comfy bed, cable TV, a full kitchen of food and human interaction.

As an eighteen-year-old, I'd often question older adults when seeking the truth behind the rumors involving her. The questions were normally answered with the old 'wink-

wink'...'at least that's the way I heard it'. The truth, of course, is rarely as much fun as the rumors.

In my little world of the dining room, guests would often shun their heads or pretend to be in deep conversation as she sashayed into our lives and started unexpected conversations on her way to a late breakfast. Going for the shock factor, she'd wave to me from only ten feet away and made sure that I saw her with a bellowing, enthusiastic *"Hello... There... Handsome!"*, but I'd be right back at her with a *"Good Morning Sunshine!"*. And to me, she was exactly that, bright sunshine in a room full of dark personalities. Her visits opened the door for me to flash a little of my own personality, instead of acting the stuffy waiter figure who was seen and not to be heard.

The Gesundburg Mansion was an old rundown, two-story farmhouse hidden from the road by several large maple trees. There may very well have been old paper currency hidden underneath a mattress somewhere inside, but you'd never guess it from the looks of the place. Each and every time that she left the restaurant after dining, be it coffee and toast or a T-Bone feast, I'd find a $5.00 bill laying near the sugar bowl. When my 17-year-old girlfriend's 17-year-old dog finally gave up and went to doggie heaven, Ms.

Gesundburg gave her the first pick from a newly delivered litter of puppies. She once gave me a car stereo for my old piece-of-junk 1964 Chevy Biscayne, not from the local Radio Shack, but from a dirty shelf in the property's small outbuilding.

Looking back at those times with a set of maturing eyes, I think perhaps that she treated me with random acts of kindness because I saw her as who she really was, which was a human being.

# Chapter Three - The Teenage Years

## *Fast Times Down the Midway*

The County Fair of my youth was a haven for quality family entertainment. Which just happened to include alcohol, gambling, and nudity. And bear vs. man wrestling. But those days are gone. The society of those simpler times has crumbled and all that we're left with now are livestock judging, rubber duckies, and cotton candy.

On the day that quality family entertainment died, Mitch and I were planning on meeting up with friends at the Fair later that evening. We were both working at the time, so the $2.00 admission fee wasn't an issue. But we could make it one. Mitch's Grandmother lived near the livestock stable end of the fairgrounds, so we could just sneak in and save the $2.00 for a greasy cheeseburger or sump'n else. Besides the guilt of breaking a Commandment, there were two obstacles to overcome to achieve entry. A four-lane divided interstate highway and a six–foot rickety fence topped with barbwire. So, after a few beers and a daily dose of "The Gong Show", we headed off to the V.I.P. entrance. Idiot drivers with reliable cars hadn't been invented yet, so crossing the interstate at dusk wasn't all that difficult. Crossing that fence wasn't as easy. Cut-off blue jean shorts were fashionable at the time, but not great fence scaling gear. As I swung my back leg over the barbwire, one evil barb pierced the skin of my upper, inner thigh. So, upper and inner, that I almost had to consider moving my singing career to Vienna and joining a different type of boy's band. But, there were no arrests and I could still spawn, so it was worth $2.00.

We nonchalantly entered the back door of the livestock stable, using the maze of animal stalls to elude a potential trailing posse of FFA members. Our actions mimicked Butch and Sundance backtracking across a small stream to create a confusing trail of hoof prints, except that our stream was cow piss.

After the clear sign was given, we headed up the midway. To the left was the all-important, concrete restroom facility. To the right, was the main grandstand area. As you passed the grandstands, on your right you'd find a realtor handing out brochures, Chuck's leather shop, and a series of food stands operated by local civic groups. If you hung out at Chuck's on the right day, at the right time, you could drink free draft beer, gamble on the trotters and eat a BBQ pork sandwich, the food proceeds helping your local community. Chuck kept a 15 ½ gallon keg of cold beer for personal consumption, hidden behind the leather chokers and wristband display. Before you could blow the excess foam off your beer, a gang of little girls would come by with baskets of numbered paper slips. One dollar, one paper slip. And you had just placed a bet on the next horse race. The mothers of the girls were the syndicate kingpins, the dads were too busy flipping burgers.

As you continued down the midway, you'd find the usual merry-go-rounds, rigged games of chance, and vomit inducing adult rides like the Tilt-A-Wheel. Located halfway down this menagerie of madness was the Number-1 midway attraction of all time. Fat Albert. Not some fat kid, but a source of entertainment, wallet-lightening, and stuffed toys. The concept was easy. A large, horizontal Wheel of Fortune had holes at the end of each colored section. Quarters were bet on the corresponding colored squares of a surrounding table. Fat Albert, a white rat, was inverted in a tin cup at the hub of the circle. The carney spun the wheel, rang a bell, and removed the cup. Fat Albert staggered/ran off to the safety of a colored hole. If the rat went down your colored hole, you won. But that wasn't the true source of the entertainment. It came from the carney himself. He graced our fair for years. Average height, slim build, dark, weathered skin. Kindda looked like William Dafoe in a t-shirt and jeans. Always with a microphone headset and sucking on a Marlboro, he was the king of the 'inside talkers'. No matter how hard you tried not to look up as you passed by the stand with your girlfriend, a quick glance was always met by his eyes, even across a crowded stream of fairgoers. And then the verbal snare took hold. With a bellowing, gravely bark *"Step right up! Place your bet! Win your girl a teddy bear! Round and round she goes! Where she stops, nobody knows! There goes Fat Albert!*

If that wasn't enough animal cruelty for one night, there was bear wrestling. The top card of the evening was a match between a drunken plumber named Jerry and a de-clawed, muzzled black bear. Jerry had the girth advantage. The bear led in the smarts department. Fifty dollars was rewarded to anyone that stayed in the ring for five minutes. Except, of course, the bear. He was probably paid in body parts.

But there existed an even Bigger draw of people to our little Country Fair. An attraction that made working in the fields all year seem worthwhile, helped bring the troops of local church congregations together in protest, and allowed many an adolescent boy to skip directly into manhood.

During this tender period of my life, I waited tables at the restaurant of a local motel. At around 10 A.M. one morning, I was alerted from the kitchen by the sound of the front door closing. In the dining room, I found two young women sitting themselves at a table. One black, one white, they were both dressed in silky tops, fluorescent spandex pants, and high heels. When I mistakenly asked if they saw anything that they liked, they both giggled and stared a hole through the crotch of my khaki slacks. I wasn't that good in math class, but TWO girls dressed like hookers PLUS Day TWO of the fair equals Hoochies. Hoochie-Choochies.

At the far end of the midway, near the entrance with a toll charge, stood three large tents. Set back off the beaten path, the tents were closer to the retirement home across the street than they were to the midway. Bright lights pulsated with the loud music, drawing dozens of men like moths to a porch light. In an unexplained phenomenon, while waiting on their husbands, the wives of the men stood around in small groups, holding the hands of their children while exchanging pie recipes and knitting techniques. In between shows, girls danced on the stage out front of the tents, helping the MC talk the men out of five dollar bills. Inside the tent was an intimate affair. Hooting, hollering, and screaming as a cross-section of the local male community was entertained by several young women wearing their birthday suits. Not that I was there. That's what I was told.

With a fine mist falling, Mitch and I stopped at a midway game to try our 'luck' at a new game. As we sipped on drinks from the parking lot bar, we handed over dollar after dollar, in hopes that the two dice would add up to a winning number. Sounds a lot like a game of craps, doesn't it? But that would've been illegal. Over the shoulder of the roller, I can see a bear slapping the crap out of a staggering man. Over his other shoulder, I see two scantily dressed blondes dancing to the Hendrix classic "Wild Thing".

And we all grew up to be somewhat normal.

## *Fear and Loathing in Daytona Beach*

(After my best friend's recent death, I figured that I would start telling the story, "The Adventures of Mitch and Robin". This was the first story that I ever shared publicly. A toned-down version.)

One evening I was dreaming about Mitch and I at the age of 19 in Daytona Beach, a trip that we took to reset our minds before the stress of months of college classes. If my brain could type, I'd have three hundred pages already.

So, here's the abbreviated story of the two idiot teenagers from Woodstock, Virginia on their big adventure to Daytona Beach, Florida.

I had worked two jobs all summer, saving money for the costs of college student living. Books, beer, and condoms. We caught the Amtrak in Richmond after having stayed at Mitch's aunt's house for the evening. It was an overnight ride to Florida. I only remember this because as soon as we had settled into our seats, we did what any normal college student would have done. *"Excuse me porter, what time does the bar car open?"*

After a good three hours sleep on a belly full of beer and no food, the train came to our stop. We got off. The train pulled away. And there we stood. Two teens from Woodstock, each with a suitcase in our hand. We were in Deland, Florida, and the road sign that we were staring at read Daytona-26 miles. Now this was 1979. We didn't have internet, cell phones, credit cards or a reservation. And, apparently, we didn't have a clue. But because good things happen to the ones that take irresponsible chances (I made that one up obviously), we noticed the well-worn station wagon sitting on the other side of the road. Joe's Taxi. We got in. Guess who was driving. A grungy looking fellow, a Vietnam veteran, who's name just happened to be Joe. He had connections at the SunRise Motel, right on the beach in Daytona. He drove us there, introduced us to the managers and left us his business card. "Just call when you're ready to head back home".

The first twenty-four hours went well. Having heard radio reports of shark attacks from the previous day, we felt pretty good about ourselves after surviving through our 3 AM Atlantic Ocean body surfing ordeal. "Especially near the docks", they warned on the radio. So, it's 3 AM, we're swimming near the big dock, there are shark attack reports, and I swim like a rock. I'm taking this one as a win.

The second evening, we did what all teenage boys do when they go to Florida without supervision. We looked in the phone book, found a taxi cab number and the address of the Shingle Shack. The Shingle Shack was nothing like the gentlemen's clubs that we had back in Woodstock. Well, that's because we didn't have such things at home. "Now, let me get this straight. Alcoholic beverages, loud rock music and completely naked women dancing on a stage. I'm in." I'm sure that during that evening, we broke every single strip club etiquette that had ever been written. But apparently, we weren't too bad because they let us in again the following evening. Yeah, we had to go back a second time to ensure that we had gotten it right the first time. We must have made quite the impression during our first visit, because after arriving through the doors the second night, the DJ hollered over the PA system *"Hey, it's my boys from Virginia!"*. Golden Ray (not her given name, I don't believe) gave us a friendly hello. After a few hours, it was time again for Crystal to make her way back onto the stage. Mitch had earlier purchased a Shingle Shack t-shirt and had Crystal grace the shirt with her autograph. Crystal was the epitome of everything that I was looking for in a woman at that point of my life. A beautiful, long-legged blonde, with a friendly smile, didn't talk too much and she was naked. Today, a handshake from a female Walmart greeter would be the highlight of my social calendar. Back in the day, Mitch and I were Mick and Keith (Jagger and Richards). He was the flamboyant, electric one, the voice of the party, while I was the quiet, sedated one in the corner. The Glimmer Twins, I was his KEEF and he was my Mick. Hunter Thompson and Raul Duke. Yin and yang. If you had ever spent any time with Mitch, you would know that he liked to talk. Our Yin and Yang. He'd ramble on and on, I'd listen and nod. So, Crystal's five minutes into her time on stage. We're sitting at stage side, me mesmerized by Crystal, Mitch turned facing me. If I remember correctly, he was repeating the same thing..."*blah, blah, blah, blah, blah*". I just nodded my head. Well, at that moment, something happened that was so memorable that I will never forget it. Crystal is dancing, facing away from us. She's positioned right in front of Mitch, yet he is oblivious. I'm nonchalantly smacking his thigh and he keeps saying "*blah, blah, something, blah, blah*". Finally, he swings his head around and comes face to face? with Crystal's rear end. And then the impossible happened. He stopped talking, the mouth gaped open, a look of confusion appeared on his face.

We were only nineteen.

If you've ever been an Olympic Games qualifying 5000meter runner, you are, without a doubt, well-versed in the different strategies taken by runners during a race. Some trail the pack at the beginning of the event, using an explosive kick at the end to achieve victory. Others battle at the front, maintaining a strong position while keeping in touch with the competition until the end of the race. And often, one runner, referred to as the 'rabbit', out-sprints the other runners right from the start, to tire out his team's competitors and/or set a torrid pace for a fellow teammate, assisting him in setting a new world record.

Somehow, the last one describes our strategy for our vacation.

We had begun our week's adventure like a couple of 'rabbits'. Out of our motel room with-in minutes of having checked in with the front desk, we had cocktails by noon, achieved a bright red 'base tan' by the late afternoon and became friends (just friends) with Krystal and Golden Ray, supporting them in their current careers, one dollar at a time. That was pretty much it, in the category of "Your first forty-eight hours in Daytona Beach". We had arrived on a Monday and suddenly it was Wednesday. Wednesday had begun like any typical day. Picture if you will, Rob and Laura Petrie, lying in separate beds, chit chatting about their plans for the day and how cute that Richie was. Ours was just like that, except that we were lying in our underwear, on top of the bedspreads, drinking scotch on the rocks, and watching the 'Roadrunner' on the television. "How can you drink scotch in the morning?", you may be thinking to yourself. It was because we had read in a Playboy magazine that sophisticated men drink scotch, a taste that's acquired over many years. We only had a few hours before an appointment with a nearby beach, so we had to hurry straight to sophistication. I did learn that a quality scotch pairs well with cheese, fruits, and pork, or in our case, cartoons. It was all quite like the Rob and Laura scenario, except for the fact that the Petries lived in New Rochelle during their five seasons on TV, whereas Mitch and Robin visited Daytona Beach for just seven days, trying to squeeze our sitcom into just one week. A long, long week.

Mitch's Grandma Rodgers and Eddy lived on the gulf side of Florida and made the trip over to visit us for a day. It was sort of like a temporary intervention by elderly angels except that we spent our time together cruising in their Cadillac, right on the beach, happy hour in their hotel room and then a well needed dinner at an all-you-can-eat restaurant buffet. In all the excitement during our first forty-eight hours, we had forgotten one little thing. Food. Dinner was as to be expected. It was early in the evening. We were taking full advantage of the 'early bird' discount, which had started at four-thirty. The restaurant had a bustling atmosphere, standing room only, hordes of ladies with blue hair, gentlemen with grey or none. During my fourth plate from the buffet, an electric, excited feeling arose from the far side of the dining room. In came EMT's with a stretcher, navigating through the waves of diners near the buffet. After vitals were checked, an elderly lady was lifted onto the stretcher, an oxygen mask placed over her nose and mouth. A moment in your life where you realize that it's not all about strippers, loud music, and breakfast scotch. That moment of reflection in which you think of your loved ones back home, the regret of not helping that homeless man during your last trip to D.C., and a renewed commitment to achieve your goal of earning a college degree, that will eventually lead to a successful career, with benefits including a wife, 2.5 children and a boatload of money. I thought of these things as we stared in silence at this dire situation. But then my bulging bubble of re-commitment was burst when I noticed that the husband of the dying woman was doing a very good imitation of a human squirrel, his cheeks bloated with food after hurriedly shoveling fork after fork of deep fried goodies into his mouth, each morsel slathered in tartar sauce or ketchup.

It was a simple time versus cost ratio. The squad would be leaving in no time at all. The buffet cost $3.95.

The next day, refueled by the fried cod fillets, cheesy macaroni, and bowls of banana pudding, we hiked our way down the main thoroughfare of town. Two young men in search of their destiny. Or a tattoo. Or just a liquor store. It's not important because destiny found us. Pimp walking down the sidewalk, we neared a young fellow. He was probably in his early twenties. Short in stature, he was comfortably dressed for the warm summer day. No shirt, cut-off blue jean shorts, flip flops, a dark tan, and shoulder-length oily brown hair. With a shady, quiet voice, he asked if we needed 'anything for the head' or maybe a black beauty to keep the party going. Black Beauty? I'm thinking Jane Kennedy from CBS sports, but he was referring to a popular stimulant pill that was readily available, illegally, back in the day. Mitch then did what he did so well. A friendly, humor-filled interrogation broke out, and little did our new friend know it, but he was the temporary prisoner. Mitch seemed to get great pleasure from, and was a master at, getting total strangers to confess things to him that they might only inebriatedly tell their best of friends. And it turns out, describing this young lad as a temporary prisoner was a pretty-close description. This fellow, with whom we just happened to run into, once rented a room above the Walton and Smoot Drug Store, main street in our hometown. He had to break his lease after he was arrested for trying to break down through his room's floor to rob the pharmacy below of any resalable prescription drugs. "Of all the gin joints, in all the towns, in all the world, a young Tony Montana walks into mine…"

Mitch and I visited the world-famous Daytona Beach Speedway, home of the Daytona 500. Thousands of fans screaming for their favorite drivers as they piloted race cars that could reach a speed of well over 200 MPH. A little hiccup in our plans. There was no race that day and the public wasn't allowed inside the massive structure. But there was a dog track next door! We grabbed a program and strutted, elbows and knees flaring excitedly, down to the track's railing. With absolutely no knowledge in the ways of the gambling world, we stared at the program for help. And there it was. Our omen to the riches that were soon to be bestowed upon us. First race, lane five, dog numbered seven..."Terrible Ted". Ted Nugent!! (Rock Icon) "Dude… dude… dude, let's place our bet!" So, five dollars were placed on Terrible Ted to win. The greyhounds are trained, after the stall doors open, to chase after a mechanical rabbit that travels on the rail around the interior of the track. With Ted and his rivals waiting anxiously in the stalls, the rabbit took lap after lap of warm up trips around the dirt oval. And then the big moment came. "Here-comes-Lucky!" screamed the PA announcer. The gates opened and the dogs took off after that metal rabbit. Rounding into the first turn, a few of the dogs became entangled. Legs and tails went tumbling towards the outside rail. Everyone involved regained their senses and loped off after the pack leaders. One of those wreck victims was, you guessed it, Terrible Ted. Ted could play a screaming guitar riff but he wasn't much of racer.

Friday began like any other day. Being marine creatures of habit, the day's activities began with breakfast beers and cartoons. Secondly, we woke up.

Mitch and I spent several hours at the beach that Friday afternoon. Just as we were leaving the sand and began climbing the stairs leading to the parking lot, Mitch started back-fist punching me flush on my birth mark, located between my left bicep and triceps. And it hurt. Now it's not that my stout, teenaged humerus bone wasn't protected from injury by mounds of rippling muscle, but I was sunburnt, dammit. And he was also trying to say something. That secretive technique where you whisper loudly through your fully clinched teeth, lips slightly parted, the speaker getting increasingly aggravated because you can't understand a word that they're saying, yet anyone watching knows that you're definitely talking about someone else. Finally, when Mitch reached a normal conversation level, I realized what he had been slowly repeating. "GGGGoldddeeen Raaayyy". Thirty feet away, standing under the outdoor beach shower, rinsing away the day's last remnants of sand, was our newest best friend, Golden Ray, the star performer from Monday and Tuesday night's visits to the Shingle Shack. Now, I take extreme pride in my uncanny abilities of observation and logical deduction. I've studied with the best of them. Sherlock Holmes, Hercule Poirot, Inspector Clouseau, Adrian Monk and, maybe most impressive, Shawn Spencer. Somewhere in the basement, I have my cherished, mahogany-framed diploma, proudly proclaiming my achievement of having obtained an Associate's Degree of Criminology, from the Cinematography School of Really-Good Detectives. It's down there, I'm going to hang it up one day, I just can't find it. I did, however, find myself staring at Golden Ray. Not the water beads forming on her young, bronzed skin. Not at the lack of material used in creating her bikini. There was something different about her and I just couldn't put my finger on it. Though I wanted to, I really did. My extraordinary skills of observation had seemed to have failed me for the first time in my young life. In my mind, I began to struggle with the reality that I may just be an average person. But then it finally clicked. The difference was suddenly obvious. She had a head. I hadn't noticed that bodily feature during our 'together time' at the Shingle Shack. It was a nice head. With hair and everything. Two eyes, two ears, and two lips. How did I miss that? Well, even Frank Columbo admitted to an occasional slip-up.

Some people might say that revealing such horrid details of our past might inspire Mitch to occasionally haunt me in the true ghost form. Memories are all fine and dandy. Something to cherish. A haunting from time to time would be welcome by me. It would be much better than not having him here at all.

## The Junkie Pad

Because of one stupid decision that I made as a young man, I went from living a wonderful existence in a tiny cabin on the banks of the Shenandoah River, to surviving day-today in a rundown old house in the middle of Small-Town, Virginia. (Edinburg, to be exact) Traded in a beautiful girlfriend, two dogs and a canoe for a bachelor's life shared with a childhood friend of mine.

The new home wasn't your everyday, run of the mill bachelor pad. In short time, it would become commonly known to many around town as "The Junkie Pad". It wasn't a shooting gallery littered with heroin needles, but it did share several characteristics found amongst other dens of sin.

Steve and I moved into this little "fixer upper" for several different reasons. First off, we didn't have anywhere else to live. The house would prove itself to be the ultimate Do-It-Yourself project, a challenge for a couple of twentysomethings with zero knowledge of home improvement. A blank canvas for starving idiots to make their mark upon.

And the most inviting incentive in signing the lease was that the rent was cheap.

Real cheap.

Like $150 a month cheap. Including basic utilities.

The house was situated smack dab in the middle of a town with a population of 752. The Hub of Main Street it was, across the road from Wightman's Grocery (the town's only) and down the street from the Post Office. It was a three-story structure, once painted white, proudly adorned with wraparound porches on levels one and two. Back in its hey-day, the home was probably the pride and joy of a well-to-do family. That would have been about 80 years earlier, at the beginning of the 20th century. But then, we moved in.

A small parking lot behind the house made for easy access to the stairs leading up to the rear entrance. A long hallway led to the door of our apartment. For $150 a month, you only got one half of one floor of one great big house. And Fort Knox it wasn't. The back door was never locked and our apartment door would barely close, no less lock. The door opened into the living room; a vast, hollow space dotted with a couple of simple chairs, a ratty sofa, and a TV set. Black and white, with rabbit ears supercharged with aluminum foil for better reception of the three available channels. The entire house had large, rope and pulley windows and ten-foot ceilings. The back third of the apartment highlighted our huge kitchen and dining area. You had two choices in getting from the living room to the kitchen. The options were walking through either Steve or I's bedroom. The one small bathroom was tucked away in the kitchen, opposite the refrigerator and our two-chair dinette set. (An aqua blue pattern, I believe) Leading down from the kitchen to the first floor, and a permanently locked door, was a grand wooden stairwell.

We moved in during late summer and THE WORLD WAS OURS. Evenings were filled with cold beer, loud music, and the giddy excitement of experiencing our first taste of freedom out living on our own. The Junkie Pad was born. It soon became a hangout for friends and strangers alike, all desperately looking for a place where they could bond with other rebels without a cause. Just up the street from us HAD been The Edinburg Teen Center, a dilapidated old building which hosted dances every Saturday night. Complete with live rock bands and a hundred of the area's youth, it was a weekly scene of sweaty young bodies, grinding and bouncing to blaring renditions of "China Grove" and "Celebration!".

The area's youth were starved for something to do. We found out just how hungry they really were during our first 'organized' party, held over the Thanksgiving Day weekend. Not the entire weekend, but most of it. Earlier on that Friday, we had told somebody to come over. They told somebody else, who apparently told a whole lot of other somebodies, who brought along their 20 closest friends. By 10 o'clock that night, there were bodies everywhere. Partyers were hanging from the balcony. The living room looked like a Rave without a DJ. My friend Anne invented couch

100

dancing.  Numerous area Fire Marshalls were waking-up sweaty and inexplicably scared.  Making the 20-mile pilgrimage from neighboring Luray was Greg S., that town's version of Keith Partridge, along with a bunch of his buddies.

Did I mention that our landlord was a Deputy Sheriff?

Our only source of heat for this great, big space was our little, inefficient kerosene space heater.  It did put out heat, but also produced a continuous plume of black, sooty smoke, which clung to everything.  Especially the ceiling.

So, the party finally broke up around 2AM and the heathens had all gone home.  Except Steve, myself, and our friend Nicky.  We were just chilling in the living room, watching a little TV, when a loud series of knocks rattled our door.  Being the mature elder of the trio, I answered the door.  Standing there in uniform were Deputy Landlord and the town's Chief of Police (the only member of the force).  Seems that there had been a few complaint-calls about loud noise coming from the general area of our living room.

*"Does it LOOK like we're having a party?!?  I can't even HEAR that little TV.  Are you sure it wasn't our neighbors?  Maybe WE'RE the ones being disturbed!"*

There's a fine line between blabbing coherent, intelligent glib-gab and drooling down the front of your shirt.

The officers retreated their way down the long, dark hallway, pausing repeatedly to convey multiple variations of *"Sorry to have bothered you guys"*. As I turned triumphantly to brag to my partners in crime, Nick calmly pointed out the obvious. *"Good thing they didn't see the ceiling."* Clearly smeared in the ceiling's thick layer of kerosene soot were hundreds of hand and finger prints left behind by Anne and her troupe of couch dancers during their premiere performance earlier in the evening.

Speaking of Anne. I've repeated the following tale a thousand times, but the first public slurring was part of my "Best Man" duties at the wedding of Anne and my best friend Mitch. I needed something 'catchy' to say to express my belief that theirs was a love that was meant to be; joined as one for the ages. Eve had the Garden of Eden. Scarlett O'Hara was the belle of Tara. When I think of my introduction to Anne, I think back to the epicenter of budding romance - "The Junkie Pad".

It was a typical Sunday morning. Nicky had crashed on the sofa overnight, which was often the case. Steve, Nick, and I were having breakfast beers, watching a muted TV, and listening to a J. Geils record on the stereo. The phone rings. It rang a few more times before anyone noticed. I answered the phone. It's Mitch, calling from his home, some 30 miles away.

*"Listen, I'm coming up there in a while. I'm bringing along this girl. I think she might be the one. You idiots try and act like you got some sense about you..."*

So, we did what good friends do. We didn't move. I can still see it in my mind. I was leaning up against the little kitchen table, wearing ripped sweat pants. Nothing else. Nick and Steve were sprawled out on the sofa. Nick was looking exceptionally punkish, with no shirt and his purple-tinted Mohawk. Steve was dressed and looking normal, except for eyes that were extremely blood-shot after a Saturday night's belly full of beer. Mitch and Anne arrived through the permanently unlocked door, all squeaky clean, dressed like preppy Ken and Barbie. We Three Sedated Misfits looked up from our muted TV, with music blaring through cheap stereo speakers, the coffee table cluttered with pizza bones and empty beer cans. But we didn't scare her off, which was the point of my wedding speech. She left later that day, but thank God, never out of our lives.

Geez, that was way too nice.

Winter was coming. Life in the new apartment had been comfortable up to this point, but now the temperatures were dropping and the winds began to howl. A few of the Junkie Pad's structural shortcomings became painfully evident as the leaves changed colors and the seasons transitioned from Fall to freezing your gonads off.

The long hallway from the outside world, with the unlockable door, was an unilluminated gauntlet that led to the apartment's entry door and served as a prototype for wind tunnel research and development. You've got your drafts, and then you've got your DRAFTS! Standing in the living room one afternoon, we checked for the source of a draft coming from the general area of the door. A half book of matches was lit and blown out while checking around the frame of the door for breezes, finally narrowing the main source of the jet spray to the large opening of the old fashion key hole.

An older, wiser person suggested stapling plastic sheets over the large rickety windows, another obvious source of cold air. Whenever a gust blew outdoors, the interior plastic ballooned like a ship's sails after the vessel had turned to catch the wind.

The observant reader may have noticed a quirk in an earlier description of the morning in which we first met our friend Anne, with me leaning against a kitchen table, while Nick and Steve lounged on a sofa, yet we all saw her at the same time. Well, there's a perfectly sane explanation for this seemingly obvious typo. It came to the point where attempting to heat the entire space of our living quarters seemed hopeless; a futile attempt at comfort and a big waste of money. There were several hot-water radiators located throughout the apartment, but nothing warm ever flowed through them. Our entire source of heat came from the sooty grates of one little kerosene heater. The first warning flare that signaled to us that a drastic change was needed, was when we began noticing the snow accumulating in the carpet of the living room. As packed snow fell off the boots that entered the apartment, it would remain there in the carpet's ugly tan fibers, clumped in its original frozen state, sometimes for days at a time.

So, we moved everything of importance from the living room into the kitchen. The ratty sofa, a few chairs, the little television, and the modern-for-its-time stereo system. Our living room had become unlivable. Ergo, the old idiom "Let freezing carpets lie." The faithful kerosene heater began its mornings in the bathroom, then spent the remainder of its day in the kitchen, napping during work hours. Our apartment had evolved into three distinct temperature zones. The frozen polar icecap of the living room and the temperate zone of the kitchen, which were separated by a third; a subclimate zone found in the two bedrooms, its average temperature leaning towards polar. We slept at night fully clothed, further insulated by three or four blankets. You could see your breath in the air that you'd exhale, illuminated by the street lights, as you settled in for a comfy night's sleep. Sleep Tight! you could, as your muscles were constricted and your mind was comforted, knowing that it was too cold for bedbugs to exist. On a brighter note, the thin walls between our bedrooms helped us in developing an Abbott and Costello-type routine, performed every workday at 6:30 A.M.

(Who's on Kerosene Heater Maintenance?)

"You up?"

"Yeah"

"You takin' a shower?"

"Nah, you go ahead. I went first yesterday"

"Seriously dude, you go ahead"

"That's OK. I smell fine. You first"

It went on and on like this until we both were late for work, then the body's temperature surpassed 98 as we scurried around getting ready.

In my younger days, I pretty much guaranteed myself a front-row seat in the burning coliseum of Hell, through different acts of rebellion and misguided stupidity. Now-a days, I return the grocery carts of old ladies in the store's parking lot and make random visits to convalescent patients in area facilities, in an attempt to secure a Visa for an eternal journey northward. I know that's not the way it works, but perhaps a handful of brownie points might help-out at the luggage-check counter.

My parents came to visit the Junkie Pad once, at the beginning of the Christmas season. Steve and I had followed holiday tradition by putting up a festive tree, the base of which provided ample space for potential gifts from Santa. But this tree hadn't been trimmed in the traditional sense. Empty beer cans adorned the ends of numerous branches. Freshly chewed chicken bones clung to the needles of the pine. And at the top of the tree, instead of an Angelic ornament dressed in white, with sparkly wings, was a pair of underwear, the sex and name of the owner long forgotten. But that day will most certainly never be forgotten. Not at least by my Mother anyhow, who still reminds me from time to time.

The large stairwell in the kitchen, which led downstairs to nowhere, was another source of the winter's chill trying to invade our comfort. So, we dove headfirst into one more home improvement project to keep 1/3 of our home toasty lukewarm. Nothing too drastic, just the best idea that we could come up with at the moment. An entire roll of plastic sheeting was stapled from floor to ceiling, enveloping the entire staircase like one great big polyethylene malaria net. A name for the monstrosity was quickly bestowed (it was so obvious). "The Boy in the Plastic Bubble". The focal point of the kitchen became the target of an ongoing, growing barrage of jokes. *"Turn that music down, he's trying to sleep."* We didn't know anyone with a malfunctioning immune system and John Travolta had to work that day, so no one really existed inside the stairwell, but it was always an eye magnet for any unknowing visitors to the Pad. Most guys would usually just go along with the running gag. But occasionally, young women would become curious and increasingly intrigued by the bubble, as the tour guide told the story with a trusting, straight face. As they slowly got closer and carefully peeked through the opaque plastic for a better view, the questions would begin.

"There's REALLY someone in there?"

"Yep"

"What's his name?"

"Don't know, never talked with him"

"REALLY?"

"Ah...yeah."

One of the bigger snowstorms of recent history blanked the town that winter. Schools were closed. Businesses shut down. Public service announcements declared that the roads were only open to four-wheel drive vehicles. We had a case of beer and some food, so being isolated from the world was no big deal. In fact, it was a blast. But then around Day 3, the beer started running low and the food was almost gone. Steve and I were friends, but after three days, we were both starting to go a little bonkers. We called our friend John. They were having a little snow-day party and invited us over.

"We'll be there in a minute!" What could go wrong?

John's place was only 5 miles away, so the unplowed road shouldn't have been much of a challenge for my '64 MGB convertible with its 5-inch ground clearance. We began our journey carrying a broom and our only shovel, heading down to the street in hopes of locating my car. I was pretty sure that it was out there somewhere, having abandoned it there only a few days earlier. Main Street had been scraped

109

occasionally since Thursday, the snow jettisoned over the vehicles resting along the curb. The only sign of the MGB was its antenna sticking out of the avalanche of snow. We laughed and cussed as we begun to excavate our chariot to freedom. In complete darkness, the streets were eerily silent, free from the sounds of machines. The only noise to be heard were the crunches of hard snow under the shoes of restless residents, shadowy silhouettes going nowhere slowly, but at least it wasn't in the living room. Two of the storm zombies stopped by our worksite.

"Whatcha doin'?"

"Goin' to see a friend"

"What, are ya crazy?"

"Yeah"

"Want some help?"

They weren't licensed counselors, but with their help, our immediate problem was exposed. We warmed up the engine and headed South on our Northern bound journey. The car jumped from the curb like a little bronco leaving the shoot at a rodeo. In front of the Phone Company, I spun the wheel and the car into a really cool 180, and off to the Great White North we went. Laughs and giggles became expletive's as we slid along Route 11, sobered by the headlights of an oncoming tractor trailer. But some things are just meant to be and we safely passed by, either on the right or underneath, it was hard to tell with my eyes closed in fear. After reaching Woodstock, a series of four attempts up side streets, which lead to the general vicinity of John's house, ended with spinning tires on the ice-packed pavement. The last failure was eased with the help of the town's maintenance crew, who probably had better things to do at the time. Finally accepting defeat, we headed back home. One more James Bond maneuver and the car was deposited back into the same icy grave from which it had risen not an hour beforehand.

Our friend Nicky was a constant staple in a home that was constantly lacking staples. Except the ones holding the plastic sheets in place. Sort of like a man's best friend; he'd blend into the background because he was always around, but he'd be there instantly when you really needed him. Just feed him an occasional beer and pat his Mohawk from time to time.

So, the usual suspected idiots were hanging around one Sunday morning, drinking breakfast beers, listening to some tunes and talking up a mess of nonsense. It was common for people to spend the night at the Junkie Pad, in lieu of drunk driving or facing the real world. In fact, various people hung out there, at various times, with or without our invitation. I remember rolling into town with Steve one night and noticing the living room lights shining bright, a beacon of no good, which was easily seen from the road below. "Hey, looks like somebody's here" is NOT the kind of thing that the normal person calmly says as they turn into their driveway after work.

But that was our normal.

Without anyone noticing, Nick had quietly slipped into the bathroom to shower. The Redskins were playing on TV that afternoon at 1:00 and the breakfast beer gang was busy sharing their expert two-cents with one another other, which added up to the equivalent of 400 worthless dollars by this point of the morning. Suddenly the madness was muted and heads turned around, as the bathroom door swung wide open. There, shrouded in a haze of shower steam, stood the dark outline of a man, looking like a rejected promotional poster for the movie "Saturday Night Fever" (another Travolta reference?). Emerging from the fog was naked Nicky wrapped in a bath towel and sporting a Mohawk full of shampoo. Before anyone could spit out a "What the...", and with his soapy hair visibly parted down the middle, Nick morphed into a Denorex Shampoo commercial. With a straight face and a puzzled look, he calmly explained to his idiot viewing audience -

"This side tingles. But this side doesn't".

Back in those days, there was only one fast-food restaurant in all of Shenandoah County. A Quarter Pounder w/cheese and some hot French fries, were well worth the 10-mile round trip for a 'special' dinner. Oh, if we'd only known just how 'special'. Steve's ugly car (a 1976 AMC Matador, scab-ooze yellow with a black Landau roof) was loaded with carbs and fountain drinks. We were halfway home when disaster struck. As I was reaching into the darkness of the floorboard, searching for my tasty beverage, a violent 'thump' impacted the car. *"Son-of-a-Bitch"* Steve screamed, as he pulled off the road. *"I think that I hit a deer...or a dog...or something!"* Steve had to follow me out of the passenger door; the driver's side door was so badly damaged that it would no longer open.

Walking back to the spot of the impact, we discovered in the far ditch, one very dead deer.

Being the law-abiding citizens that we were, sometimes, we backtracked a 1/2 mile up the road to the only payphone around (The Hamilton Motel) and called the Game Warden.

113

Well, he was off that night, so they sent a Deputy Sheriff. We met up with him back at the carcass.

Now Steve and I were 'townies'. The only thing that either of us had ever butchered in our entire lives were final exams during High School. The Deputy seemed oddly more inconvenienced by us than the deer had seemed.

*"You want him?"*

*"Sure? Sure!!"*

We grab the shattered legs of this poor animal and threw him into the trunk of Steve's car.

Which at first, seemed like a good idea. Have you ever asked yourself "Wonder what I should do, on a Sunday night at 8:00, with that dead, bloody wild animal lying in the trunk on top of my jumper cables"? Must have missed that day of Driver's Education. Remembering that our little town's only Grocery store, with its own butcher counter, stood directly across the street from the Junkie Pad, and was owned by the family of Steve's girlfriend Sharon. So, we called her brother Jeff. Shirley, he must know something about processing dead animals.

Jeff cleaned and butchered our little hitchhiking buddy, yielding us numerous steaks, stew meat and a huge mound of burger (even after he took his cut, pun intended). Now, times were lean, as was the meat, and venison had come to our budget's rescue. That night, we made cheeseburgers, the size of the 8" skillet in which they were cooked. Breakfast, for the next several days, was sirloin tips and scrambled eggs. It was nice having red meat for a change, but the sight of venison in the fridge did get a little bit old after a while, both figuratively and literally.

Yep kiddies, we walked to work each day, uphill both ways, in a driving snowstorm. Shoes! We had to share a pair of shoes! Almost had a thought of my own one day, but I had to share it with Steve. There was snow in the carpet, and we liked it. We loved it.

Just remember, Utopia is wherever you're standing at the moment. You just gotta look at it from the proper angle, with a smiling set of eyes.

Nicky, God bless him and keep him, has since left this Earth, and signed a long-term lease at a much better place up in Heaven. I can't help but smile when thinking of Nick, which is how every person should hope to be remembered.

## *Madison County – A Bridge to Cross*

One hundred years ago, I played football for the Fighting Falcons of Central High School. Early on a Friday evening, we loaded a bus with our equipment and cocky attitudes, for an hour-long journey across the Massanutten Mountains to battle against the Madison County Mountaineers, Virginia State Champions the previous year.

To appease the politically-correct crowd, let me preface this story by stating that I only hold prejudice against one ethnic group on the entire planet Earth, and that would be mean people.

The road through the dense forest of the mountains was made darker by the starless sky above. The parking lot was even darker as we unloaded the equipment from the team bus. Small groups of opposing fans shouted threats of defeat and other hostile predictions as they made their way to the football stadium.

Blue and Gold were the official school colors of the Falcons. This was an away-game, so the blue pants were topped with white jerseys, which, along with our helmets, were trimmed with blue and gold stripes. White, calf-high tube socks were in fashion at the time, with some players, including myself, even going as far as to wear white football shoes, as opposed to the traditional black. Our entire team that season had white skin.

Madison County was an hour and a million miles away from our hometown. Sure, you had your typical, good-ole white mountain boys coming out of the woods to play ball, but 40% of the Madison team that year were African American young men. We weren't used to the flip-flopped demographics and took an uneasy notice.

Steel-tipped cleats were still legal on the shoes of the players back in those days, throwing the chance of injury to the wind, in lieu of better traction on the slippery fields. We had produced a small crunching noise, like a 17th Century Infantry group, as we first marched across the graveled parking lot and filed past the angry crowd of enemy supporters.

Still confident we were, as jumping jacks and stretching exercises were executed, synchronized by the cadence call of our squad. The mounting anticipation of clashing with the opposition had testosterone pulsating through the blue and gold veins of The Falcons.

But then, our moment of manliness was rudely interrupted.

As the entire stadium of enemy fans leapt to its feet and screamed with deafening delight as they turned towards the main building, a mass of humanity left the Home Team's locker room. Clad from head-to-toe in dark blue uniforms, they emerged from the darkness, pounding fists against thigh pads, then helmets, sounding like a muscular, sweaty marching band. A third phase of impromptu percussion instruments produced a rumbling thunder, as fifty sets of steel-tipped cleats created sparks of lightening along the long trail of concrete.

The Falcons were still confident, looking stylish in white, blue and gold. Our vocal leaders rounded the troops into one large, bouncing huddle in the middle of the field before the opposing squads separated to their respective sidelines. There was no doubt in the minds of The Falcons that an upset victory would be ours before the night was through. Our arrogance was further bolstered after we won the ceremonial flip of the coin, giving us first possession of the ball. An omen of no surprise for the Blue and Gold.

The opening kickoff skidded into the end zone for a touchback. Falcon ball, 1st and 10 on the 20-yard line. Coach Lee wasn't about to lay down at the feet of a much stronger enemy, and instead went straight for the jugular vein with a daring play selection. We had implemented a new offensive system that season, patterned after the modern, explosive offense of the Notre Dame Fighting Irish. I played 'flanker', a wide-receiver that was utilized in the running plays of the offense, as opposed to only the traditional catching of the ball. My bread & butter play was "Right-25", where I carried the ball unexpectedly against the natural flow of my teammate's movements. It would soon be known around our conference of teams and by the opposing defensive coordinators, as *"Reverse! Reverse! Reverse!"* as they screamed an alarm to their troops.

The ball was snapped from the Center to the Quarterback. My teammates veered to the Right, the opposing Mob followed. I went Left and took the hand-off from the Quarterback. As I broke free from the crowd, only 80 yards of grass stood between me and a stunning, humiliating opening-drive touchdown.

Did I mention that Lawrence Young, number 20, played for the Mountaineers that season?

Lawrence stood about 6-foot-something, 190 pounds. He was a multi-sport athlete with amazing skills and a natural grace. He was a champion sprinter in Track & Field's 100yard dash, the District's leading football scorer for the second year in a row, and after high school, played major college football.

For 60-yards, my short little legs were generating an amazing RPM, my white football cleats completely clean except for the bottoms, stained from clipping the top of 60yards worth of grass. At 20-yards-to-Goal, I began to feel his presence, then saw him over my right shoulder. But my short little legs kept up the torrid pace.

Baabaa...Baabaabaa...Baabaabaa...Baabaabaa...Baabaa

Lawrence didn't run like I did. Looking over my right shoulder was like watching an Evil Super-villain, bounding in the dark from the top of one skyscraper to the next.

WHOOOSH!....... WHOOOSH!....... WHOOOSH!
Baabaabaa...Baabaabaa...Baabaabaa...Baabaabaa...Baba
WHOOOSH!....... WHOOOSH!....... WHOOOSH!

He reached for my jersey just as I crossed the goal line. Touchdown!

There were at least a dozen black, teenage female students, across the fence in the far corner of the end zone, angrily screaming profanities, making the touchdown even more enjoyable. Being an annoying, cocky, mess-with-your-mind sort of player, I scissored the football from hand-to-hand between my legs, then held it out with one straight arm, and with a flick of the wrist, spun the ball onto the grass in front of them. They got louder.

We didn't score again until Madison's 2nd-string took the field in the game's final minutes. We lost 43-12.

No matter what the game, I used to joke that "You've got to look good to play good", but in the real world, a better man always wins.

## *The Cabin*

Once upon a time, in a land far, far away from normalcy, stood a cabin in the woods. This was no ordinary cabin, but a cabin haunted by tales of teenage debauchery and immoral activities.

The cabin was known to the area's youth as simply "THE CABIN", or to some Crusaders as "MITCH'S CABIN". It was actually Fred's cabin, but fortunately for us, Mitch's Dad didn't come around very often. So, for all practical applications, it was Mitch's cabin. It was a simple structure, with four walls, two windows, two doors and a roof. Inside was a wood stove for heating and a small loft for VIP sleeping. Or if you had a girl. Furniture was of the Squatter style. THE CABIN had no public electricity or running water. A Korean War era surplus generator supplied enough electricity for a few hours of lights and music, provided there was a full can of gasoline on hand. The surrounding woods and a roll of Charmin, requisitioned from one of our homes, provided for your basic plumbing needs.

Social gatherings at THE CABIN were a self-sustaining economical adventure. Mitch was the poster child for Capitalism before Ms. Garman's U.S. Government class taught us what the word meant. For the sake of our story, a state capitalist country (THE CABIN) is one where the government (MITCH, me, and a few friends) controls the economy and essentially acts like a single, huge conglomerate, extracting the surplus value (cover charge receipts and leftover cans of beer) from the workforce (unsuspecting teenagers) to invest the surplus in further production (next week's party).

The high school graduation party of '78 was a prime example of 'our' government in action at its finest. Mitch bought a roll of generic raffle tickets and sold them to any students that wanted to attend THE CABIN party, for $5.00 apiece. Don't know how many tickets were sold or how much of the profit was reinvested for future gatherings, but I do know that the festivities got a little bit out of control.

The evening began 'innocent' enough. A dozen close friends sharing a celebratory beer and noshing on a wide variety of foods (a rarity for the cabin; the food that is). Then as darkness set-in, dozens of headlights began to appear through the trees. Eerily like the madness at Altamont, we had our goons stationed at the property's lone entrance gate, checking admission tickets, and providing an ominous show of strength. Remarks on the evening's growing attendance went from a calm, yet giddy *"Gosh, this is going well"* to Mitch screaming to me over the crowd's ruckus rendition of Alice Cooper's "School's Out". *"Holy Crap! I can't believe all the freakin' people!".* At the party's acme, a traffic jam of vehicles sat bumper-to-bumper, starting at the cabin's gate, down a half mile of graveled access road and then up a quarter mile of paved state road leading back to town. An emergency meeting of the party leaders came up with a simple, levelheaded solution. Lie. A story was concocted and spread amongst the flock of revelers. *"The Sherriff's Department has been in contact with us, warning everyone to disperse immediately. Move down to the river".* The "Warning" must have been convincing. The crowd began to retreat and headed to a familiar party spot down on the Shenandoah. We caught up with the drunken mob later that evening. A 'flash party' now occupied both sides of a half mile stretch of riverfront road;

the rural version of tailgating. Weeks after graduation, a local amateur pilot offered his own unique perspective of that night. Soaring above THE CABIN in his little Cessna 150B; "Ain't seen nothing like it before. It was like looking down at the County Fair on Labor Day weekend!"

The biggest drawback to having big parties at the CABIN was known as 'pickin' wildflowers', a morning activity that followed breakfast beers and proceeded a possible Fred/father figure sighting. The 'wildflowers' were the white and yellow blooms of toilet paper left behind at the property's edge by numerous females during an evening's party. If you were lucky, while on 'wildflower duty', all the flowers picked were pollenated with only recycled beer and nothing solid. Hazzard pay was not provided.

Days after the graduation party, Mitch and I were cruising around the streets of town when we met up with my life's first girlfriend, who was our mutual best of friend. The three of us decided to head over to THE CABIN, hang out for the afternoon and have a little cookout. Our friend (I won't use her real name Patti, because that might embarrass her if she were to read this) was going to swing by the store and pick up some hotdogs to throw on our little hibachi grill. Arriving first at the cabin, Mitch and I cranked up some music, popped open a couple of beers and readied a few lawn chairs for sunning. As any serious sun-worshiper will tell you, the best accelerant for a quick sunburn is a mixture of vinegar and baby oil. We became self-basting. As our friend's car came rolling through the gate, we had a "Wouldn't it be funny" idea. So, before the car was shifted into park, we stripped naked and reclined back in the chairs as if nothing was amiss. *"OH, MY GOD!"* She probably never noticed our dark sunglasses and straight faces. *"But...But...But...But, you said we were having a weenie roast"*.

Sundays were a day of rest and relaxation at THE CABIN. And nothing spells relaxation like sipping on a cold beer while carrying a loaded weapon. Some of our city pals joined Mitch, I, and my girlfriend one Sunday for some beer drinking and weapons training. The afternoon was spent trying to drop a 4-inch diameter tree with blasts from a 7mm Mauser rifle, in preparation of any rogue elephants that might cross the property line.

After the sun had settled behind the trees, in a strange, surreal moment, two dogs showed up at THE CABIN's front door. From out of nowhere, in the middle of nowhere, a Bassett Hound and Golden Retriever, both healthy and well groomed, made themselves at home by settling in next to the wood stove. The Rockwell scenario later deteriorated when the city hooligans placed dark sunglasses on the Hound and began giving hits of pot smoke to the two unfortunate animals. The novelty of temporary pets wore off and no one noticed their departure.

Earlier in the day, dozens of deer had been seen grazing in the cornfield down the road. A mob decision was made that night to 'go get us a deer'. Because obviously, that's just what we needed. It was pitch black outside. I had zero experience in illegal big game hunting, so I was elected the designated 'spotter', the imbelcil holding the high-powered spotlight. Kenny had a .30-06 rifle in his car and Jeff was a good shot.

Like crazed villagers heading off to capture hunchbacked Lon Chaney, we made our way to the cornfield. The spotlight revealed dozens of sets of eyes. With a single shot into the darkness, Jeff dropped a deer. We drug that poor animal a quarter of a mile down the graveled road back to THE CABIN. There was chest-beating and beer drinking. A few members of the mob drove the deer to the river for cleaning; leaving THE CABIN with a dead furry animal and returning with a Playmate Cooler of venison steaks.

We were awakened in the morning by several different men yelling *"Get up! You boys get up!"* I was lying in the loft with my girlfriend, staring up at a bumblebee trying to escape out of the window. "That doesn't sound like Fred yelling." The lethal gunshot had alerted the neighbors. The neighbors had alerted the authorities. Those two lovely dogs had led the authorities along the trail of deer blood leading back to THE CABIN. Kenny's car and rifle were confiscated. Jeff provided the award-winning quote of the morning, calmly asking the Game Warden *"Uh, can we keep the steaks?"*

# Chapter Four – Life from the End of a Pole

## *Fishing Lessons*

Back when I had my own one-man fishing guide service, I took three mentally challenged women and their mentor out for a day of fishing. The cosmetic reason for our excursion was to learn the art of fly fishing...but the ultimate, real reason was to have a great day out in nature, on a spectacular Wednesday in October, during the peak of leaf season. Not in a group home setting in Richmond, but here in the middle of God's country, the Valley in all its Fall glory.

I've got to admit...I was very apprehensive at the prospect of fishing with people with such extreme challenges. Liability issues, will all three ladies enjoy the idea, am I even capable of teaching such an elite group? The three fishermen for the day were Shirley, Linda, and Mary Lou. Shirley is a black woman, probably 63, very light skinned, short, a little stout, with a face that evokes a calm, even feeling in you. Her eyes glittered like she knows something that you don't know. But she doesn't talk too much.

Linda is a younger black woman, probably 40. Of the three, she spoke the least, but when directly asked a question to which she had a good answer, she spewed out a ray of happiness that warmed you down to the center of your heart. It wasn't clear or loud, but you knew that she was sincere in her response. Her teeth were almost gone, capped in gold and silver, and her hands were clinched with arthritis.

If you stood Mary Lou in the middle of our grocery, she'd blend right in with the locals.

Fortyish, white, long brown hair...not a person would notice that she was special until she spoke or moved. At the lake, Mary Lou reassured me more than once by saying *"It's O.K., you're a trained professional"*.

We fed the ducks at the lake prior to the required lesson. Fortunately, (for entertainment's sake), the ducks are much more professionally trained than I am. They came right up and ate the bread crumbs that I had brought along for the ladies. As I spoke of the confusing differences between fly fishing and Normal fishing, two of the three ladies stared off at the lake and the geese...as I handed them different flies, weighted and dry, they became more interested...but when I got Mary Lou up to cast, it caught the eye of Shirley and Linda...then we had a class!

There was nothing biting at the lake, so we detoured...first to the community store for a civilized bathroom break. Then off to Tomahawk Pond. We spent a very short time at the pond. Linda seemed so relaxed on the pond-side bench, taking in all the gifts that Mother Nature was offering. Relaxed is good, especially since Shirley's back cast was coming dangerously close to Linda's head. I hardly noticed because Mary Lou kept reassuring me that she was in the hands of a *"trained professional"*.

Lastly, we toured the facilities at Shrine Mont, a beautiful retreat center for the Episcopal Church. As fate would have it, the head honcho of the retreat pulled into the drive just as we parked. He gave us carte blanche up into the main building, touring the 1800circa building all the way up to the Grand Ballroom.

Bonus Coverage, as I explained to the ladies, was a short trip up the hill to the outdoor chapel. The chapel is basically carved out of stone. Seating for church services is comfortably nestled into the surrounding woods. If I was indeed Robin Hood, this is where I would have married Maid Marion.

We sat there, in the middle of nowhere. Mary Lou said that this time in the woods had lessened the strain in her shoulders that she had brought along with her from the home in Richmond. Shirley and Linda, true women of the church... sat, stared, and said nothing. I tried to get them to sing, but they just smiled. Content, relaxed, eyes gazing upon stone crosses, surrounded by trees showing off their autumn leaves, we sat there in silence.

I'll never know what those ladies were thinking.

What was I thinking? What a good day.

### Fishermen Don't Lie, Go ask a Fish

I've spent nearly one/third of my life standing in water. And typically, with only one/third of my body length submerged below the surface. Which somehow technically equates into 2711 days of my entire existence here on Earth spent holding a graphite fishing rod while trying to catch a fish. And that, for some reason, seems perfectly normal to me.

You know how your fishing buddy will say *"He was this big!"* while describing the latest trophy fish that he caught, his hand-scale getting further apart the longer the story goes on. Well, I've got a few whoppers of my own.

As a young boy, I went fishing one afternoon with my neighbor friend and my Dad. Simple bobber and worm strategy, casting off a submarine bridge. The Shenandoah is plump full of smallmouth bass, sunfish, and goggle-eye. These would be your 'sport fish'. Then you've got your bottom-feeders, 'trash fish' to most people. Carp, catfish and the slimy, rubbery lipped-so-you-can't-unhook 'em, grunting Croker style, pee-on-ya while you try to unhook 'em, fallfish. I always thought that they were referred to as fallfish because disgusted fisherman would unhook the beast, throw them up onto the nearest bank, and the fish would always "fall" back into the river, to be bothersome yet another day.

So, Robbie gets his line hung-up on something deep in the river, and with his rod bending into a U-shape, struggles to retrieve line as he cranks on the reel. Getting hooked on a rock is common when fishing a worm rig weighted with lead spilt-shot, but in this case, Robbie was making some progress as his fishing line pierced the water's surface, and was slowly coming in our direction. Probably just a big hunk of waterlogged driftwood. But then a second line appeared and as it emerged, ran taunt up out of the water to a tree limb looming high above the river's bank. Obviously, it was an abandoned fishing line that had snapped off after someone's errant cast into the trees. The limb wrapped by the fishing line began to bend as the pressure increased, and the rest of the foreign line showed itself leading back into the river's water. Robbie had his line almost completely reeled in, but was still entangled with this second line. With the first line, almost entirely on the reel, still hooked tight to the second line, there was a sudden lively movement of the second monofilament and the "real snag" became clear to us. On the end of this other fishing line, from the depths of the currents, up over a tree limb, and into the waiting hands of master angler Robbie, was a little, 8-inch catfish. That's one way to catch a fish.

But perhaps there's something to be said for this suspended-line technique that could aide in securing your next evening's supper. My friend Mitch and I spent a morning out fishing the Shenandoah as an excuse to knock back a six-pack of Heineken, the ultra-chic breakfast beer of the 1980's. He was fishing with a Jitterbug lure, a heavy floating top-water lure, painted in a frog pattern. Twenty-year-old boys being boys, it was important to our gender as to who could piss, party, and cast a lure the longest. For some reason, Mitch began to attempt to heave his lure up over a suspended swinging bridge, just to prove his 'superiority'. After about 14 attempts, the Jitterbug finally made it completely across the bridge's steel cables. Before he could stop laughing, boasting, or even start reeling, a smallmouth mistakenly took the plastic lure for its lunch. Catching a fish on an artificial lure cast over a swinging bridge hanging forty-foot above the water...try that the next time you're out on the river doing a little fishin'.

Not all 'fish stories' involve catching a citation-sized fish. Me and my future Ex-wife-to-be were vacationing down in Jamaica many years ago. And a wonderful vacation it was. But a man can only take so much hair braiding and souvenir shopping, so I negotiated with her and booked two seats on a big-game fishing boat. Just me and her, two other couples and a small crew of local fisherman. It was only $35 for a half day. After many years, I've theorized as to why this fishing trip was such an inexpensive adventure. I don't think that we actually had any hooks tied to the ends of our lines. Never had a nibble. Never landed a fish. Never saw a red snapper. Until dinnertime that evening, and that fish was swimming under a little wave of mango salsa. But I couldn't have cared less. I was boating around the Caribbean, drinking ice-cold Red Stripe beer in the company of three bikini-clad women.

Then suddenly, the Captain broke the relaxing sound of the boat splashing through calm waves, excitedly yelling to his crew, all the while pointing off towards the sea. I couldn't understand what was happening because of the strong Jamaican accents, but the crew members began directing our attention to the far side of our trolling vessel. And then they appeared. Not forty yards from ship, three Pilot whales began to surface. They flanked our boat for five minutes and then disappeared back into the deep. That $35 was money which was certainly whale-spent. Har-har, matey.

Women have natural-born maternal instincts that allow them and their young ones to remain safe, even when facing an unforeseen, dangerous adversity; giving them a second chance at survival and living on to see yet another day. Men just do stupid stuff.

So, my fishin' buddy Carey and I were out for a day of serious fishing. He's a bait fisherman. I'm a fly fisherman. The trash talk had started at our favorite bar several days beforehand, as we were planning our little mano y mano tournament which would finally determine who was indeed the better angler. The light-hearted bantering continued during our way to the river, and reached a new low as we waded across the limestone bottom of the Shenandoah. After a while, we moved past our yapping and began to concentrate solo on the mission at hand. Sure, there were little verbal barbs being thrown from time to time. *"That's what you're using for bait?... OH, that's the fish that you just caught! So sorry. My bad."* Then the fish stopped biting and time passed by without conversation, gurgling rapids were the only ones speaking as we waded downstream. Suddenly Carey starts yelling *"Son-of-a-bitch. Dammit! Youuu...."* *"What's up?"* I asked my 'hated' competitor. Seems that Carey's lure had gotten hung up on a rock and he had quickly jerked back, successfully freeing the hook from the mossy stone. But the jerk had jerked with such force, that the recoil of the line had sent the lure directly towards him and now a single barb of his three-headed treble hook had embedded itself into his right tricep. Now, we both weren't laughing at this point because it obviously caused him a lot of pain. One of us was laughing, but we both weren't laughing. We were a half mile upstream from our vehicle. So, we took a moment and discussed our possible options in caring for his injury. And a decision was made. We kept on fishing.

When we eventually got back to the car, we reassessed the situation. Carey had fished for an hour and a half with a two-inch plastic lure hooked into his flesh, so he was starting to hurt. Probably because that hook was in his casting arm. We each opened a beer and began phase two of our master plan. I unscrewed the body of the lure from the treble hook buried in Carey's arm, then trimmed away two of the treble hook's three barbs with a pair of wire cutters. "Yeah, that's better" And we headed further downstream, to a spot where Carey assured me that we'd find some really-hot fishing action.

And, we kept on fishin'.

Later, when the pain became even worse, we went to Carey's house. He had a set of Exact-O bladed tools that we could use to cut the hook from his arm. You'd think that they'd have a professional facility somewhere nearby that would provide similar procedures. Nah, that probably won't be a safe idea. Carey couldn't reach over his right arm to get the proper angle of blade on skin, so I took over. First, we numbed the surgical area with a zip-lock bag full of ice. Then like a young Christiaan Barnard, I began to whittle away at the strip of skin covering the barbed hook. I hacked and hacked, but with no visible signs of success. Carey calmly spoke up. *"Uh, it's starting to hurt again"* Why wouldn't this blade even scratch his three thin layers of skin? I carefully tested the blade against my own skin and determined one thing. The blade was about as sharp as an old butter knife. So, we re-iced and switched blades. You can't go to war with your guns unloaded. You can't attract bees with vinegar. And you can't cut open your friend's arm with a dull knife. There's a life lesson for you little kiddies to remember. So finally, the skin was sliced, the hook removed and all was well.

We met up later that evening at the Beanery, so that we could share our day's adventure with all our barfly buddies. Watered with cold beer and stimulated with dimmed lights, the story grew and grew, like many a fish story does. You want the truth. Go ask a fish.

## Fish Tales

Beautiful summer afternoons like today make me think of just one thing. Fishing. And more specifically, fly fishing. The Shenandoah River is my home body of water. Despite our efforts, it has thus far taken every punch that we've thrown its way and somehow remains a vein of life flowing through our gorgeous valley. Standing on her banks, gazing over the gentle ripples and swirling eddies, the Shenandoah gives any lucky soul an instant feeling of tranquility. The river is like a big dose of liquid muscle relaxer. The big drug companies produce their own high-priced versions. Mother Nature does it much better.

I spent most my life in the restaurant world. A world not inhabitable by just anyone. Successfully managing a restaurant requires a special blend of super-human characteristics. Most of which come naturally and are hard to be taught. Traits such as communicating well with a wide spectrum of employee and guest personalities, absorbing stress without going totally insane and somehow juggle a thousand different tasks while still maintaining a sense of humor. I often use the analogy of Robert Duvall's character in "Apocalypse Now" to describe life as a restaurant manager. Standing on the beach during an invasion of Vietnam, while bombs explode nearby, Duvall instructs two young soldiers, both world class surfers before the war, as to where the best waves are breaking off shore. As other soldiers were diving for cover, as bombs burst and shrapnel flew, Duvall stood unfazed, totally focused on his mission of getting those two boys onto the next, best, bitchin' set of waves.

Expediting in the kitchen on a Friday night would have been a challenge for Duvall's character. Calmly screaming food orders to different stations manned by the kitchen staff, timing the barks so that a family's entrees arrive in the "window" simultaneously; hot food served hot, cold food cold. Seven hundred and fifty meals in six hours. In a ticket-time of fifteen minutes or less. Many, many nights, that was how I spent the second half of my twelve-hour work day. Caffeine and nicotine were the gasoline. Cocktails were the brakes. Six days a week.

I left work early one day, a day very like today. All the conditions were ideal in allowing me to skip out of work early that day. We were over-staffed, my strongest assistant was on duty, and I had a bar regular who was an attorney, just in case I killed the next employee who called in sick or dared even speak to me.

As I frantically rushed to the river to relax, I passed a slow-moving vehicle that clogged the left lane. *"Son-of-a-bitch. Isn't she too old to be driving? Couldn't they tease her blue hair into an aero-dynamical, conical shape, to help increase her speed somewhere close to the actual posted limit. Geezy-peezy."*

It only took three steps down a muddy bank and four steps into the cool water, to bring my body to a stop and unleash two 'cracks' from my neck. I was in the town of Shenandoah, just downstream from the old hydroelectric dam. Here a river-wide series of rapids is divided by a

141

heavily treed island, which then converges into a long, slow moving stretch of water. I wore my usual wet-wading uniform. A $100 pair of wading boots, an old pair of cargo shorts and a faded Jimmy Buffett t-shirt.

I waded downstream through the rapids and arrived at the beginning of the slower section. Even before I could unleash a cast, a movement in the water to my left caught the attention of my blood-shot eyes. It was a baby otter, maybe eight inches long. He was doing the otter paddle, struggling against the slow current, apparently on his way to the river's island. When he got to within a rod's length of me, I interrupted the surreal moment by saying *"Well hello, Mr. Otter. How are you doing' today?"* In the book titled "How to Relax After Work", a quip from page 153 suggests having a one-sided conversation with an infant wild animal on their home turf. It really works.

There's an adage that goes "The grass is always greener on the other side of the fence". Or something like that. For fisherman, the saying is "The fishin's always better around the next bend". As I waded downstream, I couldn't help but gaze and wonder at the scenic area on the far side of the river. There was one long rapid, formed by a continuous limestone formation, which spilled into a calm, deep pool, a quarter of an acre in size. Framing the scene, rising from the far bank, was a huge, bare rock wall, a giant 'climbing wall', if you will. If it's worthy of a postcard, then it must be home to a trophy smallmouth.

That's the misguided logic of a hardcore fisherman. The harder a fishin' spot is to get to, the better the fishin's gonna be. So, from the easy wading conditions of my current location, I started off on a treacherous journey across the strong currents and some slippery rocks. I 'locked and loaded' my boots into the crevasses of the limestone. As my first cast unfurled, it was met at the water's surface by a loud splash/smack from the anger tail of a territorial beaver. Now I've been attacked by angry beavers before (had to go there), but apparently, I had ventured a little too close to home for the beavers' liking; especially since it was early in the year and there were probably young ones around. Speaking aloud, I apologized and begged for patience, as I retraced my slips and slides back to a safe zone. All along, Mom and Pop kept cruising from side to side of the big pool, menacingly slapping their tails against the water, despite my pleas for mercy.

So, after going a quarter of a mile out of my way to avoid a humiliating death by beaver, (Doctor, it says on the death certificate "death by angry beaver" ...Yes nurse, it's a common cause of death for men over thirty-five), I began fishing again. As I continued my trek down the right side of the river, it became unclearly obvious that nighttime was setting in. I did what any intelligent fisherman would do and began to weigh my escape options. Wade back to where I had begun or hike over to the road that paralleled the river. Now, let's see. Wading upstream against the current in near complete darkness on slippery rocks or climb through the heavily foliaged bank full of spurs and stickers and selfishly trespass through a nearly mature field of crops belonging to an unknown, possible armed farmer. So, I kept fishing.

About a third of the way in river from the bank was a large, partially submerged boulder. Like a Titanic iceberg, with its top exposed to both the elements and a shroud of darkness, the bottom blindly submerged into the depths of the river, the formation created a large eddy downstream from its permanent spot. I knew that there had to be fish holding there in the eddy, not burning energy swimming against the strong current, venturing out from the calm only to snag a bite, a crayfish or a hellgrammite, any easy meal flowing by.

I cast a large, top-water popping bug into a perfect location, nearly grazing the back side of the exposed rock. In the darkness, I saw nothing, but heard a loud 'gulp' and instinctively raised my rod tip to set the hook. Like a scene from 'Jaws", the submerged line made a stealthy cruise towards my bank. A bronzeback weighing four, possibly five pounds. (he must have been well fed because he keeps getting heavier each time that I tell this story) As he neared the calmer waters near the bank, my mind was racing. I have a waterproof, disposable camera in my vest/a Bic lighter to help see/ the fish is on a weed-less hook/ just tire him out in the shallows. And then he leaped out of the water, shook his head violently, and my trophy fish disappeared back into the dark, depths of the river. I hurriedly began casting back to the exact spot where I had hooked my white whale, the casts rhythmically timed with intervals of curses, spoken in the four new languages in which I was now fluent. Then I stopped. That big lunker was, without a doubt, hanging out under the trees of the river's bank. I started to laugh out-loud at myself.

I laughed and I laughed and I laughed. A grown man, standing in complete darkness, belly-high in water, with no convenient way back to his vehicle, incensed at not catching a harmless vertebrate which possesses a small brain.

On the way home, I was completely relaxed. I drove more like that little old lady that I had encountered earlier, than my usual, piano strung self. I took a short pit stop to my local 'watering hole'. A change of shoes, shorts still dripping wet, I bellied up to the bar for a mindless game of video poker and a cold draft beer. What a good day.

Every Memorial Day weekend, for the past twenty-odd years, my brother-in-law and his buddies have made a pilgrimage to the banks of the Shenandoah River in pursuit of enlightenment, set at a totally new sensory level. "The Camping Trip", as it became to be known, was an escape from their wives, the 9 to 5 job, and apparently away from sanity.

The ritual begins by prepping the area for service. Weed-whacking the over grown banks, setting up sleeping tents, and icing down multiple cases of beer. A huge bonfire is built and maintained constantly throughout the long weekend, employing the same basic primal instincts used by their ancestors who themselves had a quest for fire.

I had endured the festival more than once through the years, many other years not at all. On this one weekend, I had planned to visit just for the afternoon, a silly thing like employment had shortened any possibility of me going through the entire process of mental cleansing. The annual campsite is a beautiful, wooded area on the South fork of the

Shenandoah. When I arrived, about six guys had already completed the initial steps of preparation and had moved on to Phase Two. Drinking beer, shooting the empty cans with the one pellet gun available and stoking the fire from time to time. I made my friendly chit-chat with the gang before beginning on my real quest, which was to go and do some fishin'. This is a great stretch of water for doing battle with decent sized smallmouth. I walked through the field along the bank leading up to where a large steel bridge spans the river. The plan was, fish for an hour or three, then wade back downstream to the camp. I quietly inched into the chilly waters, wearing just my fishing vest, a t-shirt, a pair of shorts and wading boots. I stopped for a moment to 'read' the river and develop my plan of assault. I had fished this section of water many times before, so I knew the in's and out's, it was just a matter of where to begin. Directly below the bridge were some deep pockets that had always held good fish, but it was tough, potentially dangerous wading. Big rocks and fast water. You could venture straight out from the bank to fish a very deep hole that developed downstream of the bridge. Below that hole was a wide stretch of decent water that usually produced a good number of smaller fish. So, I'm standing there in belly-high water (back when my belly was higher), inspecting the live-action map of the river. Then, something catches my eye from under the clear waters to my left. I think that I knew what it was, but it didn't make any sense, just didn't register in the ole' noodle-brain. I raised my casting arm up to keep my fly rod out of the water (for some stupid reason, since the rod can safely get wet) and bent over face to face with the river's surface. There staring up at me from the river's bottom is no other than Andrew Jackson. Not the ex-president who's been dead now for 170 years. Don't be ridiculous. It was a twenty-dollar bill, resting quietly on the silty river's bottom, momentarily unmoved by the water's current. I stood back up, my face no doubt skewed into an expression of confusion, right eye brow raised as the lips clinch to the left. Sort of like Curly from The Stooges. My immediate thought was ...*" where is Allen Funt and the Candid Camera crew?"* I looked around, looked down at the guys sitting at our camp site, then looked back down at the sunken treasure. No TV crew to be seen, the guys seemed oblivious, and the cash was still there. Next, I had to figure out how to reach my unjust reward without getting too wet. In my fishing vest was a half-decent-quality cigar, a Bic lighter and my fishing license. I certainly didn't want any of these valuable items to become soaking wet. Plus, it wasn't exactly a warm day in May, evident by a retraction of manliness and a complete loss of desire in becoming totally submerged.

Now, it's near impossible to flick a piece of paper off the river's bottom using the tip of a nine-foot fly rod held in one hand while managing to catch the undulating money with the other hand. I should know, I tried about fifteen times. Being hard-headed and full of determination, I wasn't about to give up until I was rich... RICH, I tell you! A few different strategies ran through my head before I finally derived at the best option. The vest came off, and along with the fishing rod, was lifted skyward with the left arm as the right arm plunged for the twenty. It was mine, all mine!

A little fishing was eventually accomplished, but the giddy excitement had me itching to head back to camp and share my story. The non-fisherman had been watching me all along and were wondering what in the heck I had been doing. So, that evening, grilled hotdogs were scratched off the menu and cheap steak became the surprise dinner special. Just like I had planned it.

The following year, I had the extreme privilege of spending the entire weekend with these same Drunken Knights of the Round Bonfire. There were twenty-some guardians of 'all things manly' in attendance that weekend, including the Duke of Lighter Fluid and Sir Drinks-A-Lot. As the beer cans became empty and the fire's flames became dimmer, someone suggested the 'sure-sounded-brilliant-at the-time' idea of a fishing tournament to begin at daybreak the following day (a.k.a. a few hours from now). Tournament entry fees were collected in a ball cap and different prize categories were established. First fish, most fish and, of course, biggest fish. The first fish category was dropped because no one really wanted to get up early the next morning. There were ample canoes and johnboats available, so teams of fisherman would head up to the old hydroelectric dam and float/fish back down to camp. I slept that night with my Bro-in-law in his tent, which sounds like something that you regrettably did before he married your sister, which eventually landed you three on The Maury Show. But that's a different story. The point was that Bob woke too early on every morning of his life to get to his work on time. So, after 5 hours of sleep and 50 beers, Bob wakes up as usual, just as the sun was thinking about whether to rise yet for the day. Bob woke. Which woke me. Then we woke Jug, Bob's best buddy and the third member of our canoe's crew.

We were the first boat to the river that morning. Everyone else was still sleeping, like normal hungover human beings should be. We loaded the canoe with our fishing rods, a cooler full of iced breakfast beers and a plastic bucket for dipping the water that would eventually ooze through the small crack in the hull of the canoe. The canoe was then dragged to the bank of the river, a shallow yet fast moving set of rapids. *"What the Heck?!?"* Twenty feet out in the middle of the rapids was a big, fat carp, stuck between the rocks, half submerged in the churning water. The bottom-feeding 'trash' fish can grow quite large in the Shenandoah and this one appeared to be almost two-feet long. After getting over the initial surreal feeling of stumbling upon this big slimy beast, we went about capturing our prize. A short wade through the rapids to retrieve the fish and then chants would begin of *"We Are the Champions, my friend!"* We hadn't even gotten the canoe wet yet and we were pretty much assured the cash prize for winning the tournament's "Biggest Fish Award". We tried putting the carp into the plastic bucket for safe keeping, but he was too big to fit (*"You're going to need a bigger bucket"*).

So, the fish was secured onto a heavy duty stainless steel stringer and dangled off the side of the canoe. We dragged that poor whale of a fish down the river for the next four hours. As we encountered fellow tournament competitors on the river along the way back to camp, the story of how we 'really' caught the fish began to grow, almost as big and real as the fish itself. Jug had hooked the fish with a simple worm and bobber rig. *"Uh...yeah...that's right...he WAS using split shot to weight down the line" "He fought that fish for ten.... must have been twenty minutes" "Yep, that's how it happened. Sure was."* Later that evening after dinner and cocktails, with the award money already in hand, Jug slipped up and contradicted his own concocted story of stardom. After the 'Real' 'reel' story came out, the tournament directors convened and ruled the carp ineligible as the winner. The cash prize was returned, but never the memories.

## A Big Reason to go Fishing

The first cup of coffee and the morning's crossword puzzle went outside to the patio's picnic table to join in on the celebration of today's perfect Summer weather. Mother Nature was providing a glimpse of forecasts soon to come, after weeks of hot, humid, oppressive temperatures. The sky looked soft, a brilliant shade of blue dotted with row after row of small cotton ball clouds.

Some older Buicks come automatically equipped with a special options package, not available on most makes and models. In fact, only a few of the vehicles on today's roads offer this oh-so-sane equipment. Whenever you open the car's trunk, you'll find a pair of wading boots, a fishing vest, and a fly rod...the reel already strung with a fresh leader, tippet, and a popping bug. A lack of similar vehicles on the highways could help explain the growing schizophrenia commonplace amongst today's frazzled human race.

Just outside of town, past the Vet's office and down a steep gravel road, you'll find a single-lane submarine bridge crossing the Shenandoah River. Farm vehicles frequent the bridge during the day light hours, as they travel to and from the vast fields of crops. Parking near the bridge makes easy access for a refreshing dip in the river. Parking at this same spot in the evening is for a different reason, teenagers in lust.

The old man sitting on the bank near the bridge seemed deep in thought. His ratty old car had no hubcaps. The skin on his face was wrinkled and leathery. When ribbed about not having a fishing rod while relaxing river-side, he calmly replied "I'm just looking at the water".

Every Fall season, natural instincts kick in again for the various creatures in Mother Nature's cast of characters. Squirrels begin hording away a winter's worth of nuts. Bears stop by Home Depot to pick up supplies for their DIY cave remodeling projects. And the wise old bass of the river start feeding aggressively to pack on a few extra ounces to offset the lack of food and energy that they'll experience when the river starts to freeze-over come December.

153

The old-adage often heard in the circles of die-hard fly fishermen is "Match the Hatch". To the purist, that catch phrase means just what it says. When the fish are feeding at the surface of the river, on swarms of newly hatched May flies, you tie on a fly that matches the hatch of this insect, both in size and color. Checking the undigested quarry stuffed in the gullet of a recently landed fish can reveal other clues as to what type of fly you should be fishing. But, 90 percent of 'fly' fishing is done with lures that imitate things that don't actually 'fly'. 'Wet' flies imitate the bass's submerged dinner menu...minnows, hellgrammites, and crayfish.

The "dog days of summer" are best exemplified in the river world by the thick forests of lazy aquatic plants that flourish under the right conditions. The long strands of 'mermaid hair' are mesmerizing as they gently blow in the river's current. During periods of low water levels, the algae wreak havoc on the canoeists. But on a perfect day like today, the plants are only noticed when they break your angling concentration by tickling the backs of your bare legs.

Suddenly, the surface of the water near the bank is broken by the violent splash of a keeper-size fish. Trophy smallmouth bass will often linger motionless along the river's edge, at least until a frog or grasshopper takes a fatal last leap and becomes the mealtime's main course. It will take a precision cast to land your fly near the spot of the recent eruption, while managing to avoid the low hanging canopy of tree branches that darken the currently calm water. The planets are aligned. The cast is made. Your fly glides naturally towards the water's surface. Will the fish take your bait? Can you set the hook? What was that Really-BIG worry in your life at the moment? Oops. It got away.

## Another Fishing Lesson

I once took a lady out fishing, one beautiful summer afternoon. A day when all things of importance were remembered and the unnecessary were left behind.

Fishing to me has always been a therapeutic activity, physical by association, but often just to reset my head on my shoulders, bringing my outlook back into focus. After any short time spent alone on the water, you'll find yourself in "the zone", so totally engaged on placing a lure in the path of a fish, that the normal stream of everyday thoughts disappears. Any remaining neurons spark plans of a stealthy approach while reading the river, selecting bait to match the actual menu of the fish's diet and synchronizing the body's muscles to cast a line that carries the bait to the plate of a hungry predator. While all along never realizing that your thoughts have been further channeled by the wisps of wind, the rays of sunlight and the calming gurgles of water over rock.

On a Friday evening, through the front doors of the B&B at which I cooked, walked a couple from the city, carrying two pieces of luggage and a big desire to leave behind the strain of city life. They had stumbled upon our home with no reservations, on their way to the neighboring state for an exclusive fly fishing weekend. An escape to learn how to escape.

After breakfast in the morning, I caught wind of their plans for the weekend, the term 'fly fishing' easily heard over the popping of bacon frying and plates clanging about. Unlike a lot of people, I like to talk about things that I Do know something about and it's difficult to stop the flow of excited words when speaking as a teacher to an eager new sponge who really wants to absorb every tidbit of knowledge that I'm spewing.

Most office cubicles are adorned with pictures of family, cute children and other nick-knacks that provide the worker with a little mental escape to the outside world, with a simple quick glance up from the keyboard and telephone. The kitchen was my office and a six-burner stove was my desk. Leaning alongside the antique pie safe was a fixture unique to most kitchens, a 9" fly rod, which served as my safety rope back to the real world. For the sake of my sanity or as entertainment for guests, I'd slip out after breakfast and false cast from the back deck, a bird feeder or clump of tiger lilies as an imaginary eddy from which a big trout might rise.

The neat thing about practicing your casting mechanics with a fly rod is that it can be done in any large, unobstructed area and without a hook. A lure is not necessary because it's the weight of the line that naturally delivers the near-weightless fly, a complete reversal of the physics involved with your traditional bait-casting rod and reel.

Alica and I headed to the backyard after breakfast for improvised Lesson Number One. Which began a string of lessons over the coming months as she and her husband Ned became regular guests of the Inn. Evenings were spent learning the accompanying art of tying the flies to be used while fishing, our conversations as warm and enjoyable as the ever-present red wine and dark chocolates.

During a visit the following Spring, Alica and I headed to the backyard after breakfast for our normal post-meal casting practice. Her technique had improved immensely over the past few months, which she proudly attributed to the hours spent practicing in her own backyard up in the big city. Suddenly the rhythmic 'whoosh' of the rod's movement came to a stop and the line settled to the grass. I turned and looked at her as she let go with a sigh.

*"I've only cast this rod in two places, my backyard and yours. The line has never even touched actual water"*

So, a promise was made that day. During their next visit to town, a trip would be made to the river and her new skills would be put to the test.

I took Ned and Alica to my favorite fishing hole. Not a stretch of stream that produces vast numbers of trophy fish, but a place that I've fished 100's of times over the years. To me, it's the equivalent of putting on blue jeans warm out of the dryer or disappearing into the sofa under a big, comfy blanket. A lot of people would like to leave this Earth doing something or being with someone that they love. I'd like to be found with my rod in my hand, reclined on the prominent large limestone rock on the far side of the river, just downstream from a long stretch of rapids. Over the years, I've had conversations with all the river's neighbors. Deer nervously drinking water. A farmer's loose cow. The muskrats and I are particularly close. I know the different species of fish in the water and where in the river each type might be found.

We fished for a while with minimal results, seems the only thing nibbling was an occasional common tree limb. We had each settled into our own private comfort zones, not a word was spoken amongst our trio except for my mumbled curse words directed at another empty hook. Then Alica broke the silence.

"I GOT A FISH !!!"

From the depths of the river's current, she had landed her first ever fish on a fly. At the end of her line, panicked at the lack of water, was a little smallmouth bass, maybe six-inches in length. The content look of pride and accomplishment on her face was a heartwarming remarkable sight.

The fishing action for the remainder of the day wasn't and couldn't have been any better. We loaded up the car and began the thirty-minute journey back to the Inn. At one point along the way, the car became silent as our thoughts retreated under the surface of the Shenandoah's swirling currents. Then my eyes turned from the road as Alica broke the silence with one very memorable observation.

"That was one of the best days of my life"

Before those words were spoken, I had felt like a failure as the amateur fishing guide for the day. I had wanted and expected to have tight lines all day long, a fish caught every minute. I felt a quiet guilt after having set the bar of expectations so high.

But Alica had seen clear water while I had seen mud. It had been a carefree day, standing waist deep in a beautiful river with wonderful new friends.

It doesn't get much better than that.

## Sharks and True Love

When I hear, someone mention the term 'True Love', one thing always comes to mind. The capture and unmerciful killing of an innocent, wild animal so that one can dissect parts of the unfortunate creature to impress a girl who had 'caught your eye'. For some reason, I can never find that sentiment expressed on any Valentine's Day card in the Hallmark display. And, perhaps also, that is why I am no longer married

When I was twenty couple of years old, I made the life altering decision to drop out of college and try something totally-different. I always enjoyed driving far out into the countryside of the Shenandoah Valley, coming to the occasional stop sign, and turning left or right, for no intelligent reason. Not knowing where the road might take you, just to see where you might end up. That pretty much wraps up my life's journey thus far. Lots of folks need to have everything meticulously planned-out in advance; for fear that a decision might have terrifying results. Me and my glass half full became quite confident in my own ill-advised decisions, repeatedly fueled by the very entertaining, enjoyable outcomes. Maybe I was just lucky, but you must believe in luck for it to come true.

My good friend had the proverbial "rich uncle". I had decided to end my college career, with no solid plans for the future, no plans for the next afternoon. My friend was coming to the end of his rope of employment, aggravated at the stagnant atmosphere of advancement in the company. So, we took up the uncle on his generous offer of cheap housing, packed up a couple of things, and moved to the uncle's vacation villa in Hilton Head Island, South Carolina. Hilton Head is a golf mecca. The Island is twelve miles long, five miles wide, and ten feet above sea level. Millions of tourists leave Hilton Head each year with fond memories of frolicking on the beach or rounds of golf at one of the twenty-four public golf courses. I came away with some cool stories.

The utility bills weren't going to pay themselves, so we both succored jobs as quick as we could. I was hired on as a prep cook in a restaurant. I met a girl at work who would one day become my wife. Many years later, she became someone else's wife. A diverse cross section of humanity occupied Hilton Head. I once drank homemade eggnog at a Christmas celebration with several doctor and lawyer types, a golf course sprawling in the distance. I once manned the controls of a small Cessna airplane, the interstate transportation for a bar regular of mine, as we circled high above the beaches of the island, not a lick of training under my belt. I drank beers in the penthouse suite home to a couple of 'tennis professionals'…a.k.a. drug dealers, a dinner plate of cocaine, the size of a half bag of Gold Medal flour, sitting nonchalantly on the kitchen counter. And, after moving in with Cathy, the future wife to be, I 'sublet' my room in our villa to a fellow prep cook, so that he could stop sleeping in the restaurant's dumpster. Diversity. Yeah, that's the word.

Cathy had a friend named Chris, who had offered to take us shark fishing one day. Being a diehard, obsessed fisherman, I jumped at the opportunity to try something different to add to the angling resume. Chris was the stereotypical surfer-type that you might find hanging out on the island's beaches. Dope-smokin', hackey-sack-playin', scruffy, sun bleached blonde hair on the top of a short, tanned, well-fit body. We met up with Chris early in the morning of our little adventure, at a little bridge that crossed over one of the island's many brackish inlets. He gave us an entertaining lesson in the art of successfully deploying a cast net, to catch the day's bucketful of bait fish. Cast nets are found with a radius of four to twelve feet, with a weighted diameter edge. Both hands hold the net before a cast, the excess netting held between your clinched teeth. Then with a discus throwing type motion, the net is flung out over the water, the weighted edge pulling the parachute to the bottom, hopefully entrapping an unsuspecting school of menhaden, or a similar type of bait fish. After a laughter filled morning of trying to catch our own bait, we headed to the dock where Chris kept his boat. It was a nice size, v-bottomed, in-board motor type of boat, with simple seating and a standing accessed helm. Beer and baitfish, we were on our way.

The first eye-opening thing that I noticed about Chris's shark fishing strategy was that we were anchored within screaming distance of the beach. Perhaps the reason behind the location was so that the sunning tourists would be able to hear my screams, as the Great White Shark swallowed me whole. The focused quarry of the day would be the blacktip shark. After we had cast heavily weighted lines armed with hooks baited with menhaden, we secured the rods into the mounted holders. The three of us lounged ourselves back into our seats, two of us took off our shirts and we all cracked open an iced cold beer. I asked Chris what was next in our shark catching attempts. The answer was "sit back and wait". Then, suddenly, like that scene from Jaws, a reel began to click and fishing line left the boat. Everyone became quiet and stared at the reel. Then Chris jumped up, transformed into Curt Gowdy, lifted the rod out of its holder, dipped the rod tip forward and then with one big jerk, set the hook and the fight was on. After five minutes of battle, the tiring fish was brought along broadside. Chris drug him onto the boat's floor bottom, when magically the four-foot blacktip gained a very angry second wind. Chris started yelling to me *"Get the pipe, get the pipe!"* Mounted to the side of the helm was a two-foot long piece of copper pipe. I was to bonk the shark on the head to subdue the beast. My first attempt was probably like the sight of seeing a Catholic priest tenderly baptize a young baby wrapped in a pink blanket. "No, harder!" The spirit of Babe Ruth entered my body and I swung for the fence. The force of the strike not only rendered the shark's body to a series of involuntary muscle spasms but his left eye popped out of his head.

After our second successful catch of the day, Cathy 'proposes' the following idea. She wants a set of shark jaws as a souvenir of our big adventure. So, in hopes of a successful sexual conquest later that evening and, of course, in the spirit of 'true love', I began whittling away at the mouth of the shark, using the only knife on board, a small, dull little weapon. An easy task, except for the effects of the boat's bobbing motion and the glare of the afternoon sun. If you ever find yourself holding a set of shark jaws, freshly dissected from the head, bloody flesh still clinging to the bone, hang the jaws on a nail in a tree deep in the woods. The ants will eat away all the meat and the sun will bleach the jaws a bright Colgate white.

The nibbling of fish became scarce, so we decided to head back to the docks. Chris suggested that we make one more stop at a spot that he thought might bring us some more fishing action. Hilton Head, like any good coastal tourist trap, has boat tours circling the island so that the lucky vacationers can get a true ocean's view of their temporary paradise home. We then hooked into our last catch of the day. A good four or five-foot keeper. But then, as Chris swung the shark into the boat, the mono-filament fishing line broke free from the steel leader. The shark went berserk, flopping all around the boat's deck. Chris ended up 'catching' the shark again, this time with the bend of the large hook around two of his fingers, the heavy lead sinker holding the shark onto the other end of the steel leader. And me with my copper pipe. Like an Inuit obsessed with getting dinner for the family, violently clubbing baby seals in plain view of anyone nearby, I swung away at the shark until he no longer moved. Still on my knees, I looked up at Cathy. Not to deliver a marriage proposal, but for a sign that she knew that I would be a great provider. Then I noticed something really disturbing. A passing tour boat was lined with tourists, Ohioan or Pennsylvanian probably. Heavily lotioned sunburns, floppy hats, and sunglasses, they clicked away with their cameras, saving yet another memory to be added to the family's vacation scrapbook. I'll bet that wasn't listed on any of their travel brochures.

# Chapter Five- Observations

## *Rachel and The Little Boy*

My wonderful Goddaughter and I went to Costa Rica a couple of years ago, one of the greatest experiences of my life. She was a blossoming young woman and I was whisking her away to a foreign country. Which drew threats from her parents, Mitch and Anne. *"If you lose our daughter, do NOT come back to the United States!"* As we were unloading the family van at the curb of Dulles Airport, Rachel gave goodbye hugs to her parents and then disappeared from my sight, as she went behind the van to give her younger brother Michael a hug, in a touching moment of sibling love. I screamed *"My God! I've already lost her and we haven't even boarded yet!"*

Which I never did, so we're both still U.S. citizens.

After waking up in our temporary Paradise for the first time, Rachel and I went to the beach. Just a short walk down from the hotel. The sand at this stretch of beach was dark brown/black from volcanic rock. Lots of waves. Lots of surfers. Not for swimming. After we double-coated Rachel with 9000 SPF, she did what women do. Lay and bake, read a book. Turn over. Repeat.

I got bored after 10 minutes, but bared through the pain, constantly reminding myself that this was her special time, not mine. Keep in mind that there was a beach bar about 100 'meters' away!!! That's true love. At some point after an hour and a half or so, maturity kicked in for the both of us. We decided that we better hadn't push it on day one, being 10 degrees from the equator and looking like the only ones on the beach of a Nordic bloodline. When we first approached the beach, the road paralleled a small, slow moving river. It was basically dammed at the end by sand dunes, but managed a little trickle of a stream into the ocean. It was full of locals, instantly bringing to mind our local swimming spot, the Wolf Hole, but on a much larger scale. I'm hot, I'm sweaty. So, I suggest that we go waddle around with the little Niño's, the fat women in bikinis, and the boys and men that had apparently never before seen a tall, thin, white-skinned, redheaded young woman in a tiny bikini. Go figure. So, we're waddling, 15-20 minutes' float by. Then the surreal part of the movie begins. Behind my back, women start squealing and screaming, so loud that I was startled into instantly spinning around. Ten to fifteen feet from me, there was a small boy, two, maybe three years old. He was treading water at about 300 RPM, most of his head rhythmically bobbing under water. At first, I hesitated. It just didn't seem real. Then like a manatee on crystal meth, I headed towards him with increasing speed. I reached him, grabbed him under the arm and lifted. Within a millisecond or two, a woman took him and started smacking his back. He spits water and coughed, spit water and coughed, and then he cried. Then they all yelled at each other. Then a young girl carried the boy back out to the spot where I had grabbed him, while people yelled some more. Even I don't understand that part of the story. So, I waddle back over to Rachel. For some strange reason, the first thing that pops into my mind is *"Hey Rach...bucket list.... save boy from drowning"* (in Costa Rica, she adds). CHECK.

## *Bulgaria*

The good thing about the average age of someone having a mid-life crisis being redefined during your lifetime is that you get to have multiple lapses in 'mature judgement'. Just before my birthday a few years ago, I did what any middle-aged man would do. I purchased round trip tickets for 'one adult' on Austrian Airlines, packed a suitcase, and flew across the globe to the small, Eastern European country of Bulgaria. I didn't just spin the globe and stop it with my finger.

There was a very good reason for my destination of choice. Years beforehand, I was in the middle of my stint as an innkeeper. My cohort, Michelle, had changed course in her journey of life, leaving me one person short in a two-person operation. Not long after Michelle had moved, one sunny afternoon, there was a quiet knock on the front door. There stood a young woman, a total stranger, who eventually became my very good friend. Lucy was in search of employment. There are potentially shady companies in the world that promise housing and employment to young adults who seek to travel abroad, for the low, low price of several thousands of dollars. The shadier side of the situation is that when you travel from your homeland to the U.S., you may find your living conditions quite crude and the promised jobs non-existent. Lucy had traveled from Bulgaria to Detroit. She stayed briefly with ten other Bulgarians in a two-bedroom apartment. With no promised job to be found, she took a 24hour bus trip to meet a friend in Montana's Glacier National Park. But no jobs there led her back to Detroit. A secondhand connection with the small Russian community of Harrisonburg, Virginia somehow led her to, of all places, my front door. Some things are just meant to be.

I had jokingly threatened Lucy many times that I would one day come visit her after she had returned home. Be afraid, be very, very afraid. I always make true on my threats.

I flew overnight from Washington, D.C. to Vienna, Austria. After an hour and a half layover, a connecting flight took me to Sofia, the Bulgarian capital. In the span of eleven hours, I had left my little Small Town, U.S.A., enjoyed preflight cocktails with an Ethiopian-born bartender at Dulles International Airport, got minimal sleep at 37,000 feet sitting in the middle of a very chatty Russian tour group, and successfully passed through Australian and Bulgarian customs checkpoints, feeling nervously secure at the sight of security officers armed with semiautomatic weapons. The pounding of external stimuli had only just begun.

I eventually figured my way out of the airport in Sofia. A departure sign in the US might cheerfully read "Have a nice day!" In El Salvador, it would read "Que tengas un buen dias!" After my two years of Spanish class in high school and a year of living in Miami, I could probably guess what that means. In Bulgaria, the sign would read "Приятен ден" I was at a total loss of understanding anything written in a Cyrillic alphabet, the southern-most version of a Slavic tongue which derived from the 9th century.

Lucy was to pick me up that day at the airport. I kept checking over my shoulder at customs and at luggage pickup, but Lucy was nowhere to be seen. As I opened the doors to the main parking lot area, I was more than relieved to see Lucy hurrying in my direction. Seems that life's little hurdles had her running late. Alongside were her new husband Vasco and their 2-year-old son Sasha. We loaded into their car and headed to town.

The music on the car's radio was Classic Rock. Black Sabbath, Led Zeppelin, AC/DC. In my delirious mind, I was thinking how nice it was for them to provide me with the calming influence of familiar music. But it was just the radio. 'My music' was the music for a large cross -section of the population, ages 20 up to 60. Who'd of thunk it.

Lucy had a friend who owned a recently vacated apartment that I would be renting during the three-week period of my stay. But it wouldn't be available for the first three days of my adventure. So, she had booked me another place to act as a temporary home. On the way to this apartment, we stopped off at Lucy's place to drop off Vasco and Sash (who needed a nap), then went for a little sightseeing. At the scheduled time of 4:30, we met with the landlord of the temporary apartment. He was a little 'Guido' looking fellow, a Bulgarian mafia want-to-be. Black pants, a long-sleeved black shirt. All black clothing highlighted his gold necklace and gold watch. After he left with his signed documents, Lucy and I cracked open a couple of Zagorka beers and proceeded to snoop around the apartment.

The apartment was a nice enough place. Smack in the middle of the city of 1.5 million residents. It was on the fourth floor of a six-story building. No elevator. I had a kitchen, bedroom, and full bath. Off the kitchen was a quaint little balcony over-looking the bustling activity below and the National Palace of Culture across the street.

After Lucy left for the evening, I tried to unwind. Which involved more beers and attempting to operate the television's remote control. The remote was labeled in the English letter version of the Bulgarian Cyrillic alphabet. Which didn't help in the least. But after a while, I had the TV powered on and could manage to change channels. Quite proud of myself I was. Until I clicked up one more channel. You know how in the hotels of America, you can watch dirty movies on pay-per-view for no charge if you spastically lean your head diagonally to the left to follow the changing images on the scrambled screen. Well, this channel wasn't scrambled. Hard core porn, no ifs, ands, or butts (pauses for laughter). Well. I panicked. I thought that I had hit a pay-per-view button for "Olga Does Sofia" and I just could not figure out how to unsubscribe. I did figure out that the one button made the TV embarrassingly loud and that the next four channels were also hard core porn. I finally pushed the power button on the front of the TV and stepped away, my hands snapped back like I had just touched an electrified rattlesnake. Turns out that at 11 PM every evening, the Bulgarian equivalent of ESPN Sports Center changes its programming to adult movies until near breakfast time. That totally screwed up my TV viewing and sleeping schedules for the next three weeks.

A funny thing happened on the way to Koprivshtitsa.

Bulgaria is a nation beaming with heart-warming tradition and folklore. When I touched down in Sofia to begin my adventure, it was Baba Marta Day (Grandma March). My friend Lucy and a few of her friends whom I had never met, gave me martenitsi; red and white bands of thread to be worn around your wrist or somewhere on your person. The white represents integrity and virginity; the color of Christ. The red is the woman and health; a sign of blood, conception, and birth. At the first signs of spring (emerging blooms or the early appearance of storks, swallows, and cranes), the martenitsi are removed and hung on the branches of the flowering trees. This gesture assures that you enjoy good health and much happiness throughout the coming year. It's literally a beautiful picture, little strands of red and white hanging amongst the buds; given by one person to another person in hopes that they will be blessed with a happy, prosperous year. Even in a small village; hundreds of prays and hundreds of blossoms.

There's another custom that has a morbid origin and often drives unknowing tourists a little bit crazy, but in an entertaining way. Bulgarians nod their heads opposite of you and I when answering 'yes' or 'no'. Up and down signifies a negative response. A side to side motion is an affirmative response. According to folklore, this habit began way-back in the 15th century. Bulgaria was under the oppressive rule of the Ottoman Empire for 500 years, which suppressed the native people with evil, deadly measures. When asked by an Ottoman soldier, as a knife was held to their throat, if they were a Christian or to denounce their belief in God, a wise Bulgarian would nod their head up and down and answer in their native tongue..."NO".

I knew of this custom before the beginning of my adventure in Bulgaria, having researched extensively before the onset of my journey. But the memory of that little helpful hint apparently didn't last very long. Lucy's birthday is in the latter days of February, but a true celebration was planned after my arrival. Not for my benefit, I was just lucky. So, a dozen friends and family rented a beautiful, enormous house in Koprivshtitsa for the weekend. (On your next trip to Bulgaria, work this idea into your plans. It was SO wonderful). As everyone was settling into their bedrooms, I met Tanya, Lucy's brother's girlfriend. She was sitting alone in the large dining hall. Wanting to impress my new-found friends and show how friendly that I can be, I politely introduced myself to Tanya and asked if she spoke any English. With warm doe-eyes and without speaking a word, she calmly nodded her head up and down. Well, terrific! I unleashed into a ramble about how excited that I was to be in her country! How beautiful this village was! We're goin to have a blast this weekend! Where's the beer!? She just sat there and stared at me. Oh, that's right, she had shaken her head 'no'. She had no idea what I was saying. We never really 'spoke' again. I think maybe I scared her.

Or maybe I had been insulting. There are several things that you don't do to avoid insulting a Bulgarian. Bulgarians are a warm, friendly bunch. If you're offered a beverage while entering someone's home, by all means, take and drink!

I never had a problem abiding with that custom. I developed a running joke with Vasco, Lucy's husband, as I never refused a drink from a host. *"How do you always end up with a glass of wine, a shot of Rakia, and a bottle of beer...at the same time?"*. And I'd answer *"I'm on vacation!"* As the days went by, Vasco would raise a glass and proclaim *"I'm on vacation!"*

As we drove to Koprivshtitsa during that first 'excursion', Vasco (whom I had only just met) nonchalantly turned from his attention to driving and offered me a drink from his 1-liter plastic bottle of water. *"Why, yes, I will!"* and I took a big swig, thinking to myself what a friendly gesture that was by Vasco and, Thank Goodness I was not amongst germaphobes.

Lodging during one of our outings was reserved at a quaint, little ten-guestroom hotel owned by a friend of Vasco and Lucy. As we sat at a table in the small dining room, hungry for dinner, our waitress alerted the owner by phone of our arrival. He walked in a short time later supplied with hugs, smiles and a 2-liter former soda bottle filled with his version of Rakia. He joined us at our table for cocktails and conversation. For the most part, not understanding a single word being spoken, I just smiled and nodded. But being an old restaurant guy myself, I couldn't help but wonder what was behind the door leading back to the kitchen. I was double intrigued after dinner. The ladies had prepared a special dinner just for the three of us. Roast pork stuffed with rice and vegetables. Drinks were strong. Salad was good. The grilled bread was wonderful. And dinner was outstanding. There's only one way to finish off a meal of that quality. Strong coffee and sinful sweets.

I simply could not restrain myself any longer. I asked Vasco to ask his friend if I could possibly 'just peek' through the kitchen door. I wanted to see where a dinner like that comes from. Vasco turned and presented my request to our host. The friend began excitedly answering Vasco, his arms flaring about, his head swinging left and right. *"My God, I've caused an international incident!"* The gentleman was being an extremely proud owner. *"Of course, he can see the kitchen! We are very proud of our food!"* My little 'peek' into the kitchen turned into a full-fledged tour. I felt welcomed while meeting with the kitchen staff. One lady gave me a demonstration on how the pita-like bread had been grilled in an old, stationary iron pan. Perhaps it was the Rakia's fault, but once again, I had been completely confused and misled by a Bulgarian's unique style of head nods.

For 99% of my time spent in Bulgaria, I carried a piece of paper with me, on which Lucy had written the addresses of her home and my rented apartment. The other 1% of the time was spent in the shower. Also, written on the slip of paper were the numbers 9 12 63. That looks like a birth date, but it was instead a group of numbers very near and dear to my heart; and to my survival. That was the number posted on all vehicles of a taxi cab company that Lucy had recommended as being consistently reliable and fair. Some less-reputable drivers had the tendency to take you on a wild goose chase and charge outrageous fees. Especially if you were an English-speaking, middle-aged American.

Lost in translation: 'Dah' means 'yes', 'Ney' means 'no. You can convey your intended message by nodding your head in different directions, but the message sent depends on whether you're a Bulgarian or live most anywhere else on the entire planet Earth.

So, I'm out in front of The Mall of Sofia, hopefully on my way to Lucy's place for dinner. As usual, the cabbies are hanging out in front of the mall, devouring the never-ending buffet of shoppers making their way back home. On this evening however, I couldn't find my 'lucky' 9 12 63 taxis anywhere. I waited and waited and soon grew impatient.

Finally, I said 'screw it' and grabbed the next available taxi. What could possibly go wrong? I didn't really understand the pricing chart posted on the cab's rear seat window, so I made a short attempt to question the driver. Two things were instantly clear. He didn't speak any English and, from the dark, leathery skin, appeared to be from one of the city's scariest gangs---the dreaded Gypsy cabbies. Right from the get-go, I'm watching him with a leery eye. I sort of had a feel for the ride over to Lucy's, having tracked back and forth numerous times. We hadn't traveled four blocks when he turned onto an unfamiliar avenue. I didn't say a word. Block after block, nothing was looking familiar. I can't even read the signs, yet even they looked unfamiliar. The driver kept looking down at my 'magic' paper of vital addresses, pausing like he remembered something and then continued down road after unfamiliar road. My cab rides to Lucy's place during this vacation had averaged between 3 or 4 Lev, one way. I glanced at the spinning meter on the dashboard and it had just crossed the 14 mark. So, then we started to have an argument which neither of us could really understand. As we passed a massive row of familiar looking apartment buildings, I start yelling *"Dah! Dah! Dah!"* while shaking my head up and down, indicating "No! No! No!". He's yelling *"Ney! Ney! Ney!* while also shaking his head up and down, indicating "No, you dumb American tourist!" I finally 'won' and convinced him to let me out near the apartment complex. I got out of the cab and threw a 20 on the cab's front seat. *"Enjoy your @,@,@,@,@, money!"* I stood for a moment on the sidewalk, allowing my blood pressure to return to its normal, hypertensive level. Then I was overcome with a terrible realization. That's not Lucy's building. *"Where's my Rakia, dammit!"* So, there I stood, in a non-English speaking city of 1.5 million people, with street signs written in Cyrillic letters. Me and my little slip of paper with two addresses must have looked like a lost dog holding his ID tag. I approached a young woman heading my way down the sidewalk, praying for a miracle. Bulgarian youth are often at least bi-lingual, many speaking some English, which this young lady thankfully did. But the address was a mystery to her as well. As I started to panic, I noticed a taxi-cab parked alongside the curb a little way down the street. The off-duty female driver somehow got a message through my thick skull, "No Service". But she took a glance at my address paper, pointed off in the distance, and with broken English, said *"Only 1000 meters"*.

I flashed 20 Lev and said *"No, you take me there"*.

Finally, I arrived at Lucy's home, which provided me comfort and safety. And Rakia. Will I ever travel again to this crazy, wonderful land called Bulgaria? I think that I've finally got this straight. With my head shaking side-to-side, that would be a resounding *"Dah!"*

## Numbers

I have issues. It's a long list, as anyone that knows me well enough will tell you. And on that long list are entries numbered 3, 7, 12 and 21. Significant both as issues on the list and literally the written numbers themselves. A self-diagnosis of these issues points towards a hybrid virus of Numerology and Arithmomania. Oh, wait, Wheel of Fortune is on.

Look at the studio filled with glamorous merchandise. Fabulous and exciting bonus prizes. Thousands of dollars in cash. Over $150,000 just waiting to be won as we present our big bonanza of cash on Wheel of Fortune.

O.K., I'm back. Thanks Dustin Hoffman.

Numerology is any belief in the divine, mystical relationship between a number and one or more coinciding events. Arithmomania is a mental disorder that may be an expression of obsessive–compulsive disorder (OCD). Sufferers often feel it is necessary to perform an action a certain number of times to prevent alleged calamities.

European folklore concerning vampires often depicts them with arithmomania, such as a compulsion to count seeds or grains of rice. Which sortta explains my odd sleeping patterns and the fact that I can wholeheartedly describe the taste of blood. But that's a different issue and a different story.

I blame my cursed affliction on my Mom. On the first day of every month of my childhood, she prompted my sisters and me to utter the word "Rabbit" as the first word that we would say as we woke in the morning. In doing so, we were assured good luck throughout the coming month. Lucky rabbit's foot...get it? Yeah, it's a word and not a number, but I think that was the beginning of my condition.

My Mom's high school basketball number was 21. The number 3 was always a lucky number around our household. It just now dawned on me that there were 3 siblings. My randomly issued high school varsity football jersey number was 7. (3 X 7 =21) My randomly issued high school varsity basketball jersey number was 12. (3 X 4 = 12) (3 + 4 = 7) (12 written backwards is 21) (1 + 2 or 2 + 1 = 3) My randomly issued Pony League baseball number was 27. (2 + 7 = 9) (3 X 3 = 9) (3 X 9 = 27) My randomly issued JV football number was 18. (1 from 8 = 7) (1 + 8 = 9 or 3 squared) My birth date written in a two-digit year format (xx/xx/xx) adds up to 12.

My birth date written in a four-digit year format (xx/xx/xxxx) adds up to 22. But, but, but, that doesn't fit the numerology. Oh yeah, 22 was my randomly issued JV basketball jersey number. My one sister's birthday is the 14th. (1 from 4 = 3) April 14th (4 + 14 = 18, JV football jersey number) The other sister's birthday is simply the 3rd. September 3rd. (9 + 3 = 12, varsity b-ball jersey) (9 X 3 = 27, Pony League baseball jersey). Randomly issued, I don't think so. Mom's birthday is 12/21. Enough said. Dad's birthday is 04/19. (4 + 19 = 23, which means nothing, but the 2 + 3 = 5, my birthday) During my entire senior high school year, I set my morning alarm clock to wake at 7:12, unless my Mom woke me first to say "Rabbit".

My first girlfriend's birthday is Jan. 2nd (01 +02 = 3)

I was born 3 days later. In the same hospital.

Years ago, I read that most heart attacks occur at 9:00 A.M. To this day, I never 'sit' in the bathroom at 9:00 A.M. for fear that I'll end up like Elvis or Jim Morrison. If I grab some crackers for a snack, I take 3. If I go for seconds, I take 4 more, so that it adds up to 7. When brushing my teeth, the rinses and swallows are always in combinations of say like 4 and 3 or 5 and 2 or 6 and 1, but always adding up to the number 7.

I see one and two digit numbers in my mind as characters with different personalities. Some numbers appear in bold print, as strong stable numbers. Some are slanted to the left, some to the right, reflecting an introverted or extroverted personality. Some are flighty, some are smart. Some seem fast, some seem weak. In my restaurant management days, especially with the growing use of computers, employees were all given An Employee Number. To this day, I can instantly recall a number when thinking about an employee from the past. And the employee and the assigned number, it seems to me, somehow describe each other. Joanne T. was server number 19. Fast, on the move, but not particularly out-going. Lonnie G. was 57. Bold, brash, and outgoing. Fredericka B. (Fred) was employee number 8, a bit plain and very loopy. There was one employee, Mary, whose social security number I still have memorized. I would bet bar regulars that I knew 'every' employee's Social Security number. *"Hey Mary, come here when you have a second"*. She'd play along and they'd be amazed every time. Lunch and dinner shifts began with a fifteen minute pow-wow for wait staff, to teach new skills and go over the daily specials. Going into "Line-up", I'd have the S.S. number of any nervous new employee locked in my brain. "The fresh fish today is Mahi-Mahi, the soup is broccoli cheddar and…Susan, your S.S. number is XXX-XX-XXXX. Right? Special cleaning side-work today is dusting the tiffany lamps. The new employees would be left with a look of confusion. The older staff would offer comfort to the new. *"Don't worry, he's just messin' with you"*

Before the days of computer based inventory programs, everything was done manually. As in, a Texas Instrument calculator and a pencil with a fresh eraser. Working for a large cooperate chain, we were required to perform inventory every week. Each Sunday night, we counted all food, bar, paper, glassware, and chemical items and then extended the inventory equation by hand, deriving both a weekly and month-to-date cost and cost-percentage based on sales. It should have been enough to push someone like me over the edge of sanity. I can still recall the sixteen-different burger topping combinations from the menu. "Minnesota Fats Burger" 8 oz. burger, 1 oz. sliced cheddar cheese, 1oz. mushroom/wine sauce, 1oz. each sautéed mushrooms and onions, dollop of sour cream. A "South Western chicken" was topped with a sprinkle of diced scallions. A sprinkle was approximately a tablespoon or 17 individual scallion dices.

And the scary thing was that I enjoyed knowing these little tidbits.

Back to "any belief in the divine, mystical relationship between a number and one or more coinciding events". This past February, I had my ailing left shoulder surgically repaired. The procedure was scheduled on a Monday. The Saturday beforehand, I was creeping on Facebook and stumbled upon a picture of a young woman that I knew from the past. Her name is Samantha, but goes by the cutesy nickname of 'Sam'. On Sunday, I ran into my niece and her college buddy, also named 'Sam'. On Monday, I'm led to a private room to prep for surgery. In walks a nurse. "I'm sorry; I left my nametag at home. My name is Sam." Of course, it is. 3 female Sam's in 3 days. My surgery was performed in O.R. Room number 3. My shoulder is feeling so much better.

When I was five years old, my family moved from our well-aged, temporary home to a newly constructed house in a small neighboring town. As family belongings were being packed up for transport, a small bit of graffiti was noticed on the lowest shelf of a wooden bookcase. With a red Crayon, I had written two letters. P.i. Once our move was complete, a street address was established for our new home, the first house built in a brand-new neighborhood.

Our address became 314 Dawn Avenue. In case you skipped trigonometry and geometry classes in high school, Pi is the common spelling for the ratio of a circle's circumference to its diameter, commonly approximated as 3.14159. My Mom thought that I was a genius. Which, of course, didn't turn out to be the case. Because even I know that Pi ain't square, Pi r round.

## A Ghost Story

Once upon a time, I lived and worked at a bed and breakfast. It was a brand-new business venture for four different individuals who were dead-set on producing a product that would eventually become very, very good. A retired professor of psychology and amateur history buff, Wayne was the bank for the operation. His son Roger would be head of maintenance operations. I was the hired guru of food and service. Michele was enticed away from her homeland of Trinidad to become the Inn's Chatelaine, the lady of the house.

The Inn is a restored mansion (circa 1855) and stands four stories proud. There are ten guestrooms, each with their own bath. Beautiful woodwork, original fireplaces, and a wraparound deck, romantically adorned with a wall of rose bushes. It was quite the undertaking.

The Inn's original owner was named Audrey.

The first step in our new venture was getting the house ready for guests. Wayne and Roger spent their days on landscaping projects and other aesthetically-pleasing features. I painted all ten guestrooms, each a different color from the Civil War Era palette. Michelle worked on handcrafted curtains and the sort, adding a lady's touch throughout the home.

One Saturday morning (the day of my ghost enlightenment), I was in the basement, the first floor of the house. I had an office 'area' set up beside my little apartment room. My other three Musketeers had left for the day, leaving me to myself. All alone. In that great big building. I was checking e-mails and working on Web site promotion, when something dawned on me. Why am I working while the rest of the gang is off playing? Well, I'd do a few more things and then kick off for the rest of the day. But my competitive spirit got the better of me. The Ashby Room needed just a mattress to become the first guestroom completely readied to receive guests. What a heap of guilt I could hold over the others if I could simply move a queen-sized mattress from the first floor up to the third floor. By myself. My hardheaded self.

I slid the mattress to the bottom of the basement stairwell. This was going to be the hard part of the journey. Utilizing the weight of my beer belly and the never-lose mentality of my caveman brain, I forcefully bent the mattress into a u-shape that conformed to the angle of the rickety old basement stairs. Up ten more steps and leg one of the journey was complete. I slid the mattress over to the landing of the grand staircase that led up to the third floor. A queen-sized mattress was not going to defeat the king of furniture moving. After twenty-five minutes, forty stair steps and three heart attacks, we had arrived at our goal of reaching the third floor. I leaned the mattress against the hallway wall and began a well-deserved 'king of the mountain' break. Just as my mind questioned *"where in the heck is my open can of lemon-flavored, Lipton Iced Tea"*, the mattress fell from its resting wall onto the top of the stairway's handrail. My drink, which had been sitting on the top of the handrail, fell through the open gap of the winding stairwell, and landed with a clunk on the floor below. *"Son-of-a-bitch!"* A sweetened beverage spilling across the original hardwood floors. What kind of reward was this for my 'above and beyond' efforts? I stomped downstairs to assess the damages. Despite a few drops splashed across an area throw rug, the undented can sat ominously upright. *"Geez, that's kindda weird."*

After lunch, I plopped my tired, achy body back in front of my computer desk. You know that feeling that you get when someone walks behind you, you can't see them, but you sense that they are there. I got that feeling and it came from the older section of the cellar, fifteen feet or so from my desk. I looked over my shoulder and saw nothing, my attentions returned to my desk work. The feeling happened several more times over the next twenty minutes. So-strong of a feeling that it led me to red wine and out the basement's back door. It's a beautiful afternoon, there IS no one here, and I'm a grown man. Go back into the house, silly.

Audrey is buried in the cemetery just down the hill from the Inn. It is rumored that during the latter stages of her life, she had developed a brain tumor or cancer. The medical experts of the time determined it to be a mental illness and she was confined to an institution up north for the remainder of her lifetime. She loved her beautiful estate and vowed to return home one day.

As far as I can tell, after days of research on the subject, you have three categories of ghostly, undead spirits. Casper, the friendly one. A murdered Patrick Swayze, romantic ex-lover type. And lastly, the Amityville Horrors situation, were you develop red welts on your chest after being levitated two feet above your bed, your husband sees an image of a man

191

with his head blown off, and your daughter develops an imaginary friend named "Jodie", a demonic pig-like creature with glowing red eyes. I was hoping that Audrey was friends with Casper.

One morning around 7 AM, my Caribbean princess Michelle comes strolling into my kitchen domain. Eyes very wide open, she asks if I had watered the hanging plants in the sitting room. The only plants that I had ever watered were the bushes out by the barn that I had pissed on. Seems that after an evening of being 'alone', the plants' baskets were dripping water all over the handcrafted window seats.

In the same sitting room one day, I had joined a gentleman in conversation as he waited for a friend to join him. We sat on opposite sofas; my line of sight over his left shoulder was of the butler's kitchen and its open folding door. As we chitchatted about nothing important, I watched as the folding door slowly closed. I politely excused myself because I had just remembered that I had a very important errand to run. It ran from that sofa to the back yard. He was paying to be there, so that's where I left him.

A loud boom had Michelle and I running from opposite ends of the Inn to a spot near the laundry room. We triangulated and found the source of the noise. A 2 gallon,

Costco brand container of liquid laundry soap had fallen to the ground from its resting place above the washing machine. Could happen to anyone. The vibrations of a commercial sized washer spinning a full load of linens could easily have been the cause. Problem was. No linens. Not spinning. No reason.

I once hosted an afternoon tea for eight local women. I spent my morning creating different scones, cookies, and crumpets. Standing facing the kitchen's oven, I spun around after the startling crash of the gallon container of vegetable oil that had knocked open the pantry's door from the inside. As I told the story to my ladies' group, one lady jokingly suggested that Audrey was hinting that a recipe had needed more oil. (Wait, or was that a back handed insult from that old lady? :)

Doors slam and floors creak.

It's just the nature of an old house.

As I gave tours of the Inn to newly arriving guests, one question would occasionally be asked. *"Are there any ghosts?"* My blunt reply *"Do you want there to be any?"* To the interested, I presented Audrey's story, which grew more elaborate over time. To the rest, it was room keys and breakfast times.

And the following happened more than once with un-Audrey-knowledgeable guests. As they entered the breakfast nook in the morning, they'd stop and ask *"Do you have ghosts here in the Inn?"* Michelle and I would look at each other and laugh, then slowly ask the person a drawn-out *"W. h. y?"* Seems that during the night, they had the overwhelming feeling that someone was sitting in the chair at the foot of the bed, staring at them as they tried to fall asleep.

We didn't have a set time for breakfast. One Sunday morning, all our guests had eaten, checked out and departed. Except for one young couple who didn't come for breakfast until almost 10:30. As we patiently waited as they enjoyed their meal, a loud series of obvious footsteps crossed the bedroom floor above us. Michelle and I looked at each other and we began laughing nervously. Someone had to go check and see who was up there. I was busy banging skillets around, pretending to cook for a dozen new guests. But there weren't really any new patrons for which to cook. Or was there? Being the spirited soul, Michelle gladly fell for my antics and up the stairs she went. But, of course, no one was there.

Once we were host to a sweet, elderly couple who spent the entire week with us. The husband didn't get around well, so when the wife wanted to go explore the town, Michelle would sit and talk with the old man. Entertaining him for hours with her usual warmth and grace. At the end of the week, after settling-up their tab, the gentleman pawed through a wad of cash, looking for something extra to give to Michelle as an expression of gratitude for her attentiveness. I don't know the final gift, but the man became insistent that he should have a ten-dollar bill among his huge roll of paper currency. The couple bantered back and forth about the 'missing' ten, in a loving way like many old couples do. The four of us searched up and down the stairs, and then throughout their guestroom, never finding so much as a penny. Finally, there were hugs and handshakes. And on their merry way they went.

After all the guests left us at the end of a busy weekend, there would be a ton of cleaning and laundry to begin. I still had a kitchen to clean that weekend, but tried to help Michelle with stripping beds. We were up and down the stairs for hours, from guestroom to laundry room and back again. The house seems extra quiet after the crowd would leave us and you'd find yourself deep in thought as you went about the inglorious part of inn keeping. I was snapped out of my trance by Michelle. Her beautiful smile always made me laugh and in the King's best English, she began accusing me of something that I 'must have done'. After countless trips over the blue, eight-foot Oriental rug that graced the grand stairway's landing, she had noticed the green ten-dollar bill lying there on the rug, for the entire world to see.

It wasn't Michelle. It wasn't me.

There was no one else in the house.

Or was there?

## *An Empty Circle*

The cool thing about traveling the country for a big cooperate chain of restaurants is living in different cities and meeting thousands of different people, then skipping town after five or six months, all the while experiencing something new on each and every day. There was one 'typical' deployment that was spent down in beautiful Savannah, Georgia.

An obvious downside to this nomadic movement was exactly that, the movement. For almost ten years, my camel was an automobile loaded down with clothing, some pictures, and a fishing rod. The other, bigger drawback to the constant change, even though I did meet some wonderful people along the way, was never establishing any long-term friendships of any kind. The longest relationships in that ten-year span had nothing to do with two marriages, but were with people who were doing just what I was doing, moving anywhere, and doing anything to catch that leprechaun and his pot of gold.

The day before my departure from Savannah just so happened to be my birthday, the twenty-eighth I believe, but I not too sure (the haze of the road). The restaurant's staff understood it was my last day of work there, and then on top of that, the word got out about it also being my birthday. By the end of another exhausting twelve-hour shift, the offers of "First Drink's on Me!" became constant, almost to the point of comical. Now, my Mommy taught me good. It would be rude to visit someone's home and turn down a free meal. In this case, the free meal just happened to be an assortment of liquor shots chased with draft beer, but that's close enough to proper etiquette.

Cary was one of the first of the wait staff to finish her shift that evening. She grabbed a stool at the bar and let it be known at all within earshot that she had saved me the seat next to hers. My hectic day was ending as well and I joined her a few minutes later. As unprofessional as it now seems, it was common practice for employees to congregate at the bar after work. The only rule in place at the time was that the employee had to remove any obvious connection to the business itself, like a logo-ed server apron or kitchen ball cap.

For the manager-types, it was simply removing the neck tie. So, I slipped the power tie from the collar of my perfectly pressed starched shirt, just as the parade of "Happy Everything!" drinks began appearing in front of me.

I was in Low Country, coastal Georgia and Cary could have easily been the Belle of the Ball over at Rose Hill Mansion. She was a petite, pretty, young woman, with long golden locks and porcelain skin. She was immaculately groomed everyday and spoke with an elegant Southern drawl.

*"I certainly am going to miss you"* whispered my little Scarlett O'Hara.

I was trying to think of something really Rico Suave to say as I slammed back the first of several B-52's, when the breaking of glass and screams of angry men spun everyone's heads around facing the general area of the salad bar, which was proudly displayed near the front entrance and showcased 100 pewter dishes filled with a variety of freshly prepared salads, including multiple vegan options and 8 homemade dressings. But that's not important right now.

What is important was that the locally-based Army Rangers had been 'discouraged' from visiting every single bar in the entire city of Savannah, except for two. And ours had a salad bar. One of our regulars had been the sixth soldier off the first helicopter during the Invasion of Grenada. They wore t-shirts inscribed with motto's such as "Land Softly-Kill Hard". They were my buddies. But for some reason, there was an on-going dislike between the Rangers and the Townies. The Townies were exactly like the Rangers except that they had head hair, pick-up trucks, and shitty attitudes. And apparently, they didn't like sharing their girlfriends with the men in uniform.

So, after sprinting in the direction of the ruckus, I suddenly found myself in the middle of a four/now five-person choke-hold, filled with punches, blood, and cursing. The Ocean of Anger finally separated, long before the MP's scheduled nightly visit and all things returned to normal. Nightclub normal.

I took my testosterone and climbed back onto my hooch throne. The long-sleeved shirt was now missing its top two buttons and the left rolled-up cuff was smeared with someone else's DNA. The abandoned layered drink sitting in front of me was chugged with a heavy sigh of relief and my attention returned to Cary.

Robin Lambert

*"I'll never forget you"* she said, the pitch of her voice now elevated by the excitement of the moment.

Yep, that was a day in the life of a traveling restaurant manager. Cary and I never saw each other or spoke again. The circle remained empty

# Chapter Six- The Medical Chart

## *The Elephant Man and His Bruised Ego*

A funny thing happened in the Emergency Room one morning. At least it's funny now, it wasn't particularly funny at the moment.

For an employee of a restaurant, the world can be a dangerous, painful place. Slips and falls, broken glass, sharp knives, and some serious equipment with the sole purpose of cooking, grinding, and slicing raw meat. Inanimate commercial kitchen equipment are equal opportunity providers, they don't care whose raw meat they process. During a life's work spent in many a kitchen, I've seen more than my fair share of lacerations, severe burns, and broken bones. And that was sitting at the bar after work. The kitchens were really dangerous.

Electricity powers a certain percentage of the kitchen's equipment, but most of the bigger pieces' function by burning natural gas. The deep-fat fryers, stove tops, and ovens have a pilot light, burning most of the time, so that the cooking temperature can be quickly increased and adjusted. But every once in a while, somebody's got to re-light that pilot light. There were several times during my younger days, due to poorly designed or malfunctioning equipment, or stupidity, when I singed the hair from my eyebrows or right hand and forearm. No big deal, when you're young.

Skipping ahead in the medical file of past injuries; it was around 9 o'clock on a sunny Tuesday morning. Shortly after someone had 'cranked up' all four gas ovens used in baking that day's luncheon special, it was discovered that the oven on the far left had quit working again, no pun intended. Occasionally, with the back door opened for a delivery truck, a strong breeze would blow-out the pilot light in that particular oven. Someone would have to re-light it.

*"I'll take care of it!"*

WHAT COULD POSSIBLY GO WRONG?

Whoever designed this model of oven should have been burned at the stake. The pilot light was located at the bottom of the oven, hidden behind a decorative steel panel, about midway into the oven's depth. All you had to do was lie on the floor, reach up with your left hand and continuously press in a safety- 'primer' button, while stretching your right arm, which held the wind-resistant lighter, through a 5-inch space which was protected on all sides by sharp metal edges. Then hold that pose for 35-45 seconds.

After four or five attempts that successfully began with a lit pilot, only to fade back to darkness, I gave my aching butt and back a rest.

Never lacking determination, my break from full-contact yoga was quickly over. After assuming the position, I gave it one more try. Seems a malfunctioning oven-part was slowly leaking natural gas into the cavity of the oven while I had been resting on the floor.

Ever see the movie 'Backdraft' with Kurt Russell, where they have those really-cool special effects with balls of flames exploding through doors and windows? Yep, that's what it was like. Co-workers screamed, I cursed, and off to the ER we went.

As the nurse turned, while assuring me that the Doctor would be right in to see me, she asked if I would like something for the pain, either a pill or a shot. Yes, please. After twenty minutes passed, and still without any pain relief, I reacted to ANY sound of movement near the privacy curtain by lifting my trash bag full of ice cubes from my face and abruptly, politely screaming *"PAIN PILL!"*.

Shortly after the Doctor arrived, so did the Fire Marshall. Perhaps there had been a rash of other church-affiliated businesses cooking up crack as part of their tax-exempt status. Notification by staff is in fact the law with any similar reports of explosions.

The afternoon was spent self-medicating. Pain pills and margaritas. I slept well that evening, likely due to the emotional stress of the accident. One big concern of the Medical staff was the possibility of permanent damage to my eyes. So, throughout my overnight opiate/alcohol induced stupor, I was to apply a thick, creamy medication, with my finger, directly onto my eyeballs. Have you ever noticed how no one does that as a hobby? There's a reason. I couldn't use my index finger because it was wrapped in gauze after being severely cut as I quickly withdrew my arm from the ball of fire. Like Bruce Lee quick.

In the morning, I felt my way to the bathroom. I faced the large bathroom mirror but couldn't see myself because my eyelids were crusted over, despite the random streams of oozing creaminess. After prying apart my eyelids, I began to inspect the peeling skin of my face and lack of hair on the usual places. My facial skin fell off in clumps, transplanting itself onto the bathroom's sink.

I was to return to the hospital later that morning for a follow-up with the Doctor and meet with an eye specialist for hopefully good news. Clueless Alicia Silverstone was the receptionist on duty that morning. After being asked to fill out the normal paperwork, I explained that I'd need a little help and perhaps she might assist me.

*"Oh sure. Name?*

*Address? Emergency contact?"*

She then glanced up from the clipboard and said,

*"Extent of injury…Let's see, it's a laceration of your Right index finger?"*

*"And My Face!"* I wailed through lips swollen with pain, causing me to look and sound a lot like John Merrick.

*"Oh, and your face is burnt?"*

Later, the Doctor tried to humor me with an analogy of how women in Hollywood pay thousands of dollars for a chemical peel with similar results, and mine only took a millisecond. I'd have laughed if it didn't hurt so much.

I am not an animal! I am a man!

With really-soft skin.

## *Roanoke*

On the drive-back to reality.

After spending a month in a hospital, after falling extremely ill, I was transferred to another facility for a month's worth of Physical Therapy.

The transport ambulance had been 45 minutes late for the 3-hour drive to the convalescent home. And, on top of that, it was raining. Neither of the drivers seemed overly concerned, continually chit-chatting about things that had nothing to do with patient care. It's a weird, uncomfortable feeling to be lying on a gurney, exposed to the world through the large rear window of an ambulance, a constant flow of heavy traffic first tailgating, then passing you by, as you head off to what would become your temporary home for the next month. Not really knowing what to expect at this facility.

Not knowing what was expected of you. I had been hospital bedridden for a month up to this point, going from near death and thoughts marred by hallucinations, to a slightly fuzzy grasp of reality.

We unloaded at the back of the building, in the dark, only pole lights to show the way. It certainly didn't seem an appropriate setting for my Grand Entrance. I was paperwork processed, then wheeled to a bedroom. Again, everything seemed so dark. We had arrived late in the evening, well-past dinner time and all the other patients had been settled-in for the night. My 'surprise roommate' was out like the lights and I was reassured by the Nurse that he 'wouldn't make a peep until morning', which struck me as odd. The roommate was indeed a surprise because my insurance had provided for a private room. After I had questioned the room arrangement and some fact checking was completed, I was moved to an equally dreary room, but this one without a living corpse sleeping next to me.

Darlene was the first name that I remembered amongst the staff members whom impacted me during that long month of October. A thirty-something African-American with a constant smile and perpetually positive attitude, she was a large woman, not obese, just big. Both in stature and presence. When I asked about the possibility of getting something to eat after first arriving, she smiled *"Dinner was over a long time ago, but let me go see what I can scrape up for ya"*. After September's month's-worth of restricted hospital food, she returned with a plate of baked ham, scalloped potatoes, and collard greens seasoned with fatback. I'm pretty sure that this meal came from home, the personal food that staff had brought in, because future meals came nowhere close to this delicious dinner.

At this point in my recovery, I could stand on my own and scooch my feet a few steps at a time, but was otherwise restricted to a metal-walker for mobility. After that first day's long journey, it was such a relief to be lying in a semi-comfortable bed with a belly full of food while watching a little television. But, then I felt the urge for a different kind of relief. During the first few days of my stay, a trip to the bathroom meant that a call for assistance was required, not because I wasn't hard-headed enough to get there, but because the staff freaked out when I removed the different monitoring wires myself. I know this all too well because I tried it several times. It's not just a male-ego thing, but it's very humiliating to need and be required to ask for help in doing something so basic. When the monitoring wires were finally done away-with for good, I was free to travel to the bathroom on my own, which presented me with yet another problem. I had been offered multiple times and urged to ask for help during bathroom breaks. There was even an emergency assistance cord at the base of the bathroom's wall. But my male-ego/personal pride/strong desire for independence wasn't going to have any part of rational thinking. For any visits that required sitting, I could easily get my butt to the toilet, but even pulling on the towel rack directly in front of me wasn't getting me back to my feet. So instead of asking a nice person for help, I practiced, somewhat successfully, the art of toilet dive-bombing. It's very sad (and frustrating) when one of your biggest short-term goals in life is improving your potty technique.

The bathroom was shared with the adjoining room. I never saw or heard from him during our entire four weeks as roommates. Seems that all his bodily wastes were collected with different plastic tubes and bags, I never even saw him leave his room. Before coming to this facility, with its good reputation as a physical rehabilitation center, my foggy brain had images of a Gold's Gym full with buff, young people recovering from sports-related injuries. I feared being an embarrassment to myself in front of them. Then Darlene asked me a question on the second morning, as I was wheel chairing my determination over to the therapy room.

*"You're not a lifer, are you?"*

The clues were all there, I just hadn't put them together yet. The patient demographics didn't include any young, physically-fit Gold's Gym members. At 55, I was a decade or two younger than most of the other residents. For a significant percentage of the residents, this was going to be their very last home, sweet home. Some weren't aware of it, some didn't admit it, but a few that I spoke with, told me as part of matter-of-fact conversations that 'this is where I'll be for the rest of my life". Being around some of these sad souls had a Death Row-atmosphere type of feeling, but without the protesters outside, and these lifers had done nothing wrong.

For most of my working life, I had been, at bare minimum, a semi-professional in a professional world. Rules, regulations, and checklists were a normal part of the old 9-5. Early-on during the first week of my stay, I saw two gentlemen pass by my room several times, one morning after breakfast. They appeared to be Professional types, with their clipboards, sense of urgency, and personas that screamed *"Yes, we are busy (nod)… that's nice…We'll get back to you on that little matter later…we're a little busy right now."* Secondly, what struck me as being odd about them, was that they both were male. Except for the dish room area in the kitchen, which I never saw, there were approximately 4-5 males on the entire payroll, two of which were holding clipboards. The older of the two gentlemen was the newly appointed Director of Operations, and this thorough walk-through was to ensure that everything was 'ship-shape'. After 900 years spent working in the restaurant industry, one's 'eye for detail' gets honed to the point of obsessive behavior. A few minutes after the guys had excused themselves into my room *("We'll just be a minute, we're busy")*, I couldn't keep my observations to myself any longer.

*"Hey, why isn't there a clock in this room?"*

*"Ooo, good point. Mark, make a note of that, we'll have maintenance take care of that"*

There's a lot of time spent noticing things when you're confined to a bed, sixteen hours a day. The high-light of everyday was when Anyone walked into the room. Anyone. I perfected the art of electric bed adjusting within just a few hours. Being an old food service guy, I would take a mental note of the time on my new clock as the food carts came rolling down the hallway, and then calculate how long it would take until they were served to the rooms. The patients didn't, but a restaurant would have gone belly-up. Terrible ticket-times. All the metal hooks on my privacy curtain had their little clasp-openings facing in the same direction, except for three in a row, which were annoying me, above my head, to the right, starting at the fourth hook from the wall.

On the way to therapy one morning, at this point still without a clock on the wall, I decided to stop off at Mark's office and offer another one of my acute observations.

*"Sorry to bother you, I'm sure that you're busy. I can get my wheelchair in-under the hand sink in my room, if I move the trash can. But when I'm brushing my teeth or attempting to shave, all I can see in the mirror is the top of my head."*

Granted, my room had apparently been converted into a patient room, but you'd think there'd be some regulation on the check-list about this, like a common-sense law.

And so, began my road to recovery. And now, from our home office in downtown Mars, is tonight's "Top Ten List". The category is "The Top Ten Things that I took away with me from my nightmarish hospital experience":

10. Geez, this is no way to live.

9. After being tube fed some strange-looking substance, I'll never look at Quaker Maple and Brown Sugar Instant Oatmeal the same way again.

8. I hope that nurses aren't allowed to Instagram while on duty.

7. Hospital workers are wonderful people.

6. Falling out of bed a few times will get you a "Fall Risk" bracelet. No cash prize awarded.

5. The towels aren't worth stealing.

4. If you're really bored one afternoon, go visit a patient in an old folks' home. They're really bored and feeling hopeless. Believe me.

3. You can't have your dignity and modesty surgically removed. They can, however, be quickly wiped away by male hospital attendants as they clean your own excrement from your soiled rear end.

2. If you tell the dietician that you WILL NOT be here for the rest of your life, it seems that you get bigger portions.

And, the Number 1 thing that I took away with me from my nightmarish hospital experience...

If you're lying in the I.C.U. and you don't see any bright lights or pearly gates, it's because God still has another purpose in keeping you around.

Don't know what it is yet, but the anticipation is killing me.

## *Melanie*

Ten months ago, I went to the Shenandoah Memorial Hospital to make an appointment for my first of many Physical Therapy sessions. After completing the usual paperwork, an appointment date was set. The lady who was helping with the formalities wrapped things up by saying *"You'll be working with Melanie, you're gonna like her"*.

Being the male pig that I am, my first thought was that maybe she was a massage therapist originally from Sweden and had just begun a new career after her days with the Bikini Team. But insurance doesn't cover that apparently. Having the receptionist predicting "you're gonna like her" with such certainty struck me as odd. Well, I should have asked her for that night's lottery numbers, if I'd only known that she really could see into the future.

I've been jokingly calling the past twelve months "The Continuing Saga of the $1.38 Man". We have the ability! We can rebuild him! But the truth of the matter is that these past twelve months have really sucked the big one. Nine days from now will be the One Year anniversary of me entering the hospital for a two month stay that almost killed me, in more ways than one. Therapy at SMH began next, originally for a constantly painful coccyx, and then right into post-op therapy after surgery on my left shoulder. I was coming down the home stretch of recovery when I injured my right knee, which was operated on last week.

Between the weeks spent bed-ridden in a hospital, to chasing constant pain around different areas of my body, through session after session of Therapy, then hours on my own spent at the hospital's gym trying to rebuild my body, I've had a Whole lot of time to think.

I can easily name and see the faces of thirty people that attended to me over the past twelve months. But that'll be a story for a different day. Today, September 3rd, is about Mel, for two very good reasons. The men and women that work in the Medical Industry are human. And most are Super-Human. They spend their lives relieving the pain from patients like me who they themselves can be a pain. As I lay in bed or as I sat on a stationary bike, I developed my own little case study of those wonderful people that I had met who have dedicated their lives to helping others.

Case study subject Number 1. Melanie.

Standing five-foot nothing, my first impression was that of a little, compact, glowing ball of energy, exuding confidence through a pleasant smile and a quirky sense of humor. Not two weeks into knowing this young woman did I ask her "Have you ever seen 'The Silence of The Lambs?'" Now, being compared to a country gal turned FBI agent seeking to capture a serial killer, by employing the help of a psychopath who cannibalizes for dinner, probably isn't wayup there on the list of 'Flattering Things to say to a Woman'. But my connection was this. The movie's heroine, Clarice, came from humble beginnings, excelled in her career through dedicated, hard work and could speak in an intelligent, meaningful manner; untarnished by the twang of her Southern accent. It was like Clarice personified, except a conversation might begin with a silly knock-knock joke, followed by an understandable explanation of the extreme atrophy in my left shoulder.

A few weeks ago, I was proudly telling Mel of how I could feel a noticeable improvement in the mass of my once-pitiful shoulder muscle. She reached out to touch and assess for herself. If a stranger did that to you, you'd probably flinch instinctively. But I didn't give it a second thought. Not at least until half way during the short ride home, when I found myself chuckling at how much I naturally trusted my little 'Miracle Worker'.

But Mel isn't the only one working in the Rehab facility. She's more like the ringleader in a circus full of healers. There have been many a day where it really hurts to get out of bed. It hurts to get into my car. But I still do both and drive myself to the hospital's gym. All the therapy isn't physical. A lot of it is mental. There's always an air of enthusiasm, encouragement, and hopefulness at the gym. The only contagious thing floating around that department is self-improvement. When I drag my sorry self to the gym each day, I'm motivated by not wanting to let them down. They want me to get better, so I'm dedicated at getting better.

I'd have to imagine that patients sometimes become numbers to the hospital staff. And the patients sometimes perceive hospital staff as irritants to their own aches and pains. Recuperating patients may not always show their appreciation for the dedicated work of the hospital worker, but they're thinking it. Trust me. We talk. I might not say so directly to the staff, but I try to show my gratitude by delivering homemade baked goodies from time to time.

The two reasons to make this gibberish about Melanie? First off, she's made a gigantic, positive impact on my life during this past year. And secondly? It was written on September 3rd, her birthday. Hey, Mel! Happy Birthday!

## *It's Death at the Door*

During my senior year of high school, a friend of mine choked to death on his dinner. He had begun to feel ill, excused himself from the family dinner table, went to the upstairs bathroom and proceeded to choke on his own food until he was no more.

I was the typical 'popular guy' in high school. It was a time in life when I was a leader by example, a teen that other teens may have looked up to. In the movie of Tony's death, my character would have stepped forward as a source of strength to others, a shoulder on which to cry. The protagonist who speaks deeply profound, inspirational words that would comfort the broken hearts of others.

But I hadn't read the script. I cowered instead. Buses were made available to shuttle students from the high school to the Catholic Church on the day of Tony's funeral. I do remember that I went through the entire book of excuses looking for a reason not to board one of those buses. But to this day, I have no recollection of whether I got onto a bus or not.

218

I don't like death. It's no fun to be around. In retrospect, it was kind of funny when our family swordfish, Sally, did one final full gainer onto the living room carpet and was discovered by my sister, who promptly startled the family awake with her blood curdling screams. I do understand the concept of death. Or the multiple concepts, as it seems. I don't like funerals. I have no real place for death anywhere in my life at this moment. Perhaps later, at a more convenient time. I've faced the real possibility of my own death on multiple occasions throughout the years, but I was always determined to be ineligible at the time.

But why this phobia of death? Or perhaps even a better description, a dislike of death. I don't really fear my own death, I just don't like being around anything that involves the concept of death until my own moment of departure.

As a toddler, I was very close with two of my grandparents. So-close in fact, that we literally lived together on the same property of land. They both died between the time that I was born and the day of my fifth birthday. I've often wondered if under a licensed hypnotic state, a glaring mental blockage would be unveiled, leading the professionals to say *"Ah, ha, I think that we have our answer!"* I have no memory of either one of their funerals, but my Mom tells the story of how I had once asked her a question after visiting their gravesite. "But who's going to feed them cereal in the morning?"

The different religions of the world have varying viewpoints about death, but every religion acts as a tool to their followers in accepting death as a natural part of life. You got your Hindus and reincarnation, which seems to be working out well for the nation of India, with the enormous number of people and cows. You got your 72 virgins waiting for you in some versions of the Koran's explanation of 'Paradise', which sounds cool, unless you're a woman. Then you only get one man, and "the woman will be satisfied with him". The math just doesn't seem to add up here for some reason. The Tibetan Buddhist and the resolution of grief seems like a neat idea at first, your deceased love one being left at the top of a high mountain to rejoin nature. But then you read further about the exotic sounding 'sky burial'; how your body will be cut up into little pieces by the priests and left for the vultures to devour. So, I'm sticking with Heaven and Hell.

The last visual memory that I have of my other set of grandparents, together in the same room alive, is an extremely emotional, stunning vision, almost like a famous painting on display in my mind. But it provokes sadness within me at the same time. My Grandma had always been the epitome of the strong, country woman. Fixing dinner for the clan, picking fresh flowers to grace the windows of her front porch, attending church every Sunday. And there she lay, withering away due to illness, my Granddad sitting attentively, devoutly by her bedside. A picture of love.

Years ago, in my only close attempt at fatherhood, little Andrew died in the womb. The mother carried our dead son in her belly for several days until the doctors determined that it was both necessary, and safe for the mother, to have labor medically induced. When asked, who is stronger, Man or Woman, I'm voting woman. I don't know how she did it. On the one year anniversary of Andrew's 'birth', I had me a little pity-party. There were only two guests invited. Myself, and a 1.5-liter box of cheap, red wine. At just around midnight, on the back patio of my house, something comforting happened to me. The sky was mostly clear and the stars were twinkling. The glow of this evening's full moon highlighted the outline of the occasional cloud. And just as I was about to take my sorry self to bed, I looked up at the full moon once more. A cloud, the shape of your typical Christmas Tree Angel, slowly floated towards the moon. You know, symbolically heading in the direction of

Heaven. I'll swear on a Bible this to be true. I went inside the house before ever seeing what happened to the cloud, simply because I didn't want to see it disappear into darkness.

Years ago, my best friend gave me a book to read. It was entitled "No One Here Gets Out Alive". It's about the life and times of The Doors lead singer, Jim Morrison, the rock and-roll icon. The book is divided into three sections. "The Bow is Drawn" "The Arrow Flies" "The Arrow Lands" It's a great analogy of the tragic story of his life. From humble beginnings, then soaring to superstardom, and finally falling back to Earth. My friend, who gave me this book, passed away just a few years ago. We had led a slightly similar lifestyle to Jim throughout the years, apart from multiple groupies and No. 1 gold records.

My arrow hasn't landed yet. It fell back to Earth recently, but safely skidded across the dirt, leaving me with memories of my dearly departed loved ones and comforted by the strong faith taught to me as a child. I'm not finished here on Earth quite yet, but it's nice to know that there's something special in which to look forward.

## *With Thanks*

The Christmas season was hard on the Old Man. The past year had not been kind and his mornings were spent creating a reason to have felt useful by dinnertime. It was part of a vicious circle of which he had become both proficient and emotionally drained from. The passing of friends or family members no longer came as a shock, his clean suit hung readied near the front of the bedroom closet.

Between moments of concentrating on the morning crossword puzzle or taking a sip of warm coffee, his thoughts would battle with each other over the value of his existence and the hopeless possibilities of the future.

The deep rut that he had dug for himself looked down at him from a hundred feet above. Hung on the walls were dozens of old memories cast in dusty frames. To stare at a pleasant chapter of his life's story helped to momentarily set his mind at ease, only to have it snapped-back to the present by the worthless feelings that refused to let him go.

Today needed no busy-work created to provide for the dinnertime feeling of usefulness. Thursday at 2:00 PM, the week before Christmas, was the scheduled time for yet another Doctor's appointment. One personal quality that hadn't lost its edge over the years was his sense of humor.

*"Going to extremes to get healthy for some reason that even I don't understand. Makes perfect sense."*

Most of his jokes were told only to himself, so he laughed at some things that only he would find amusing.

As he dressed for the trip to the hospital, he sat on the edge of his bed and put on an old pair of comfortable shoes. It had become a running gag with himself, at this point of the day, when he'd turn his attention from the tying of shoe laces to a glance up at the top shelf of his closet. There, lying under an old, blue tote bag, was a family heirloom, a long-barreled 22-caliber pistol, and some old ammunition.

*"Well. There's always that option."*

And then he'd laugh to himself. That was never really an option, there were still a few loved ones around that he'd never hurt intentionally. But to say something to himself that would be so alarming if mentioned in a crowd, is what made the tasteless joke so darn funny to himself.

As he passed through the inner door of the Doctor's office, the receptionist glanced up and recognized him with a smile. As she opened the small Plexiglas window with her left hand, her right hand reached for something on the desk.

*"Today, I'm also the delivery person! Your little buddy told me that I MUST give this to you when you came in today."*

The Old Man thanked her, as his mind flooded with questions. He already knew the answer to Who.

*"But Why? When? Where was she?"*

As he walked around the corner to his appointment, he became the excited little boy from a Christmas Eve many decades ago.

*"I wonder What it is?"*

Throughout his last year of constant trips to the hospital to improve physically, there was one Young Woman who occasionally played a part in his treatment. Her part eventually turned out to be of enormous help mentally, not physically. Her efforts could have been seen as a complete waste of her time, but not to the one Old Man, the one who was healing. She first caught the eye of the Old Man for the obvious reasons. She was young, beautiful, and full of energy. He was an Old Man, but he was not dead to the sight of something so attractive. But over the course of dozens of chance conversations, a respect grew for the psyche of this Young Woman, as did the hopes for his glance to catch a smile from her, even if only just a passing one.

The Old Man was elated by the excitement in her voice, as she spoke of the hopes and dreams in her future. Furthering her education. The highs and lows of her workday. The highlights of family vacations. It made him feel worthy and of value when she'd ask for advice or an opinion. As with any lonely soul, when given the chance, the Old Man told tale after tale of his past, the Young Woman always attentive. Her attentiveness was proven genuine and his self-esteem further bolstered, when she recalled details from stories that he had told weeks beforehand, or politely deflect his apologies, as he began to tell a story for a second or third time, as old men sometimes do.

He began to slowly realize, as he prepared for each new day, that the holes in his life, his gripes and moans about everything, seemed temporarily filled by her presence. A conditioned response, if only for a few moments each week.

The Old Man had once misspelled her name. He had, more than once, spoken inappropriately to the Young Woman and had confessed on multiple occasions, dark secrets, and sins from his past. But she didn't run.

Occasionally, after he had confidently given sound-advice on how others might straighten-out their troubled lives, she'd throw the advice right back in his face, reminding him of how his advice, in fact, might help his own troubled cause. Bruised momentarily, he slowly learned from her that she was right.

The Old Man had made many a mistake in the past, but he was not stupid. This Young Woman was learning a profession that would help improve the lives of a rotating cast of characters, over an indefinite length of time. And he was but a member of that cast. Time to grow up and move forward.

As a teen, the Old Man had developed his own simple tenet by which to live. If he could make just one person smile, once a day, imagine the impact that he could produce over a lifetime. Nowadays, the catch-phrases with similar philosophies that float around the social circles are "Pay-It Forward" or "Random Acts of Kindness". But the Old Man had forgotten how to cause his own little ripple effect upon the world, until recently.

The gift from the Young Woman sat unwrapped on the desk of the Old Man, from Thursday until Christmas morning. Not under The Tree, because there was no tree.

He glanced over at the gift periodically throughout those four long days. The gift was wrapped in silver paper, printed with Season's Greetings worded a hundred different ways. The subtle handwriting of a woman addressed the tag. To hold the gift in his hand, it was obviously a book. It was in fact, the greatest story ever told. Not the words yet to be unwrapped, but the story of her kindness that surrounded the gift.

The Old Man spent the remainder of his life forever grateful to the Young Woman, rediscovering the joy of giving and its unknown powers of change within others. Deep in his heart, he hoped that the smile that she had given him, would one day find its way back to her.

And (Ann), the Old Man was once again himself.

# Chapter Seven- Dear Mitch

Many people remember my friend Mitch as "The Man, The Myth, The Legend." The life of every party. The extrovert who made such an impression on so many lives.

But as you may have already guessed, the point of this next little story is to show the other side of my friend that touched so many lucky souls; some lives improved without them even knowing it.

The following is an actual e-mail that I received from Mitch several years ago. Call me crazy (You're Crazy!), but I've kept dozens of his old e-mails, never daring to delete them. Just something else to hold onto, trying to remember better days gone away. Heck, I even have his e-mail address still in my list of contacts. So many times, I've thought about replying to old e-mails written by him, or sending him a new message of my own. But I'm afraid to try. Not because he might answer my message, but because he might not. Silly, I know.

Date: Friday, February 1, 2013 3:00 P.M.
Subject: 3rd Grade at Woodstock Elem.

First.......I have never told another grown-up this story. (Mitch, you have now. Cupcake)

I get off the phone at work and both Rachel and Michael were bitching about classmates. I wrote them each a letter but enclosed this story.

In Mrs. Watson's 3rd grade class we had a dirt-poor classmate named xxxxx xxxxxx. Her parents obviously shopped at the thrift stores and took clothing handouts. They sent her to school wearing such clothes. I can only imagine that her home life made Les Miserable look like The Great Gatsby. Everyone teased her.

We were told to bring in shoe boxes and the next week during art we would turn 'em into Valentine's Day mailboxes.

All the kids had fun making their mailboxes. Mom bought me a pack of 30 5X10 Valentines with envelopes. I thought to myself "to hell with my classmates". I grabbed a year book just to remember all my classmate's names and addressed 30 envelopes all to xxxxx and signed each classmate's name. For the next 5 days, I slipped 5 to 7 envelopes into her mailbox.

I can still remember the look on her face when she opened her shoe box and had 31 Valentine's in it. (One from Mrs. Watson).

Anne said the letters I sent to R & M made them cry.

You know 43 years later it still makes me too.......

Mitch

~

Yep, I know the feeling...

# Just a Guy

# Telling Tales

www.ingramcontent.com/pod-product-compliance
Lightning Source LLC
LaVergne TN
LVHW041213080426
835508LV00011B/939